The Historical Dimensions of Irish Catholicism

Emmet Larkin

The Historical Dimensions of Irish Catholicism

The Catholic University of America Press
Washington, D.C.

Four Courts Press • Dublin

Published by
The Catholic University of America Press
620 Michigan Ave., N.E., Washington, D.C. 20064
and in the European Community by
Four Courts Press
55 Prussia St., Dublin 7, Ireland
Email: fcp@indigo.ie

Printed in the United States of America

The paper used in this publication meets the minimum require-
ments of American National Standards for Information Science—
Permanence of Paper for Printed Library materials,
ANSI Z 39.48-1984.
∞

LIBRARY OF CONGRESS CATALOGING-IN-PUBLICATION DATA
Larkin, Emmet J., 1927–
    The historical dimensions of Irish Catholicism.
    Reprint. Originally published : New York: Arno Press, 1976.
(Irish Americans)
    1. Catholic Church—Ireland—Addresses, essays, lectures.
2. Ireland—church history—Addresses, essays, lectures.   I. Title.
BX1503.L37   1984   282'.415   83-23175
ISBN 0-8132-0594-8

A catalog record for this title
is also available from the British Library.
ISBN for Four Courts edition: 1-85182-305-0

To my good friend
Lawrence J. McCaffrey

Table of Contents

Introduction

In the spring of 1975, my good friend Lawrence McCaffrey, while enjoying a short holiday with our families in Brown County, Indiana, suggested that I should consider reprinting a number of my articles on the Roman Catholic Church in Ireland in the nineteenth century in the series he was then editing for the Arno Press on *The Irish-Americans*. He explained that he thought a reprint of a collection of my articles would prove very useful in arriving at a better understanding of that most interesting phenomenon, Irish Catholicism, which became so important a part of the religious landscape of not only the United States, but everywhere in the English-speaking world in the nineteenth century. After some further discussion, I suggested that perhaps my two articles published in *The American Historical Review*, and a third that was about to be published in that journal, might be appropriately reprinted in his series under the title of "The Historical Dimensions of Irish Catholicism." At the same time, however, I also expressed some serious reservations about the first of these articles, which had been published in 1967 and which would have to be modified or revised in the light of the scholarly research in Irish economic history since that date. Professor McCaffrey then proposed that I write a brief introduction to the three articles, explaining the extent to which they had been modified by either recent scholarly research or further reflection on my part. I agreed, and the result was the appearance, with an appropriate introduction, of *The Historical Dimensions of Irish Catholicism* in 1976. Because a great deal of what I wrote in that introduction some

1

eight years ago is still useful in explaining the genesis of these articles, I trust the reader will not take it amiss, if I repeat to some extent, at least, what I said then.

No one who has read anything about modern Ireland, or who has lived there for any length of time, can have escaped the fact that the Roman Catholic Church in that country is a very powerful and influential institution. The power and influence of the Church in Ireland is formidable because she is at one and the same time a political presence of no mean proportion in the ongoing constitutional system, a social institution that permeates nearly every aspect of Irish life, and one of the most powerful economic corporations in the country. In understanding the role of the Church in modern Ireland, however, the real question has actually less to do with the fact of her power and influence, which is obvious, than with how and why she has been able to acquire that power and influence. Indeed, it may not be too much to say that no history of modern Ireland can be written, nor any understanding of the dynamics of Irish society today be come to, until the how and the why of the Church's power and influence in that society has been fathomed.

In introducing these three essays, however, I should also explain that while they are certainly an attempt to come to terms with the questions of how and why posed above, they are also a function of the fact that there is no history of the Church in Ireland in the nineteenth century, and that I have for some years been engaged in the researching and writing of such a history. Because that history is now projected at some ten volumes (1780–1918), these essays were a necessary preliminary to the conceptualizing of that history. The chief problem, of course, in writing a multi-volume history is how to maintain perspective. Each volume in itself may remain whole and constant, but the volumes taken together may add up in the end to no more than a series of disparate monographs. The ideal solution to the difficulty perhaps would be to complete all the volumes and then proceed to rewrite them in terms of the general themes that had emerged. Such a solution, however, is obviated not only by the fact that academic exigencies and professional ego seldom allow for septuagenarian *magna opera*, but by the even more deadly constraint that the great work may never be completed. The difficulty might be partially remedied by proceeding chronologically, but that remedy imposes its own limitations in terms of logic and consistency in the developing presentation. Because I have chosen, in any case, to proceed idiosyncratically in the writing of my history, and the sixth volume, *The Roman Catholic Church and the Creation of the Modern Irish State, 1878–1886* (1975), has actually been the first to be published, followed by the seventh, *The Roman Catholic Church and the Plan of Campaign in Ireland, 1886–1888* (1978), the eighth, *The Roman Catholic Church in Ireland and the Fall of Parnell, 1888–91* (1979), and the third, *The Making of the Roman Catholic Church in Ireland, 1850–1860* (1980), I have to some extent, at least, avoided the pitfalls of such a chronological approach. This procedure, however, while mitigating the difficulties by not compounding them, has not contributed very much to the critical problem of maintaining perspective, and these essays, therefore, are the result of an effort on my part to see the Irish Church at least whole, if not constant, in the nineteenth century.

Because the first essay in this volume on the growth of the economic power and influence of the Church in Ireland in the nineteenth century was written some twenty years ago, something should be said about the extent to which it has been modified by more recent research and thought. When the essay was written, in fact, Irish economic history was still in its infancy. Since then a considerable amount of very good work has been done, which has certainly caused me to reconsider some of my earlier assumptions with regard to the Church's role in Ireland vis-a-vis both capital investment and economic growth.[1] Twenty years ago I argued that the Church inhibited economic growth in Ireland by diverting a significant amount of the capital available for investment to its own uses. My assumption then, of course, was that there was a shortage of capital. Professor Joseph Lee, however, has persuasively argued in a number of articles that what hampered economic growth in Ireland was not a deficiency in the amount of capital available, but rather that it was not used in an intelligent and productive way. Both he and Dr. L. M. Cullen, for example, have pointed out that bank deposits increased in Ireland in the latter half of the nineteenth century. They rose, in fact, from £8 million in 1845 to £60 million in 1913. Lee and Cullen have also pointed out that the continued increase in livestock numbers after 1830 is yet another indication that there was no shortage of capital, at least in terms of agricultural development, and that indeed Ireland was a net exporter of capital for much of the nineteenth century. In a word, the main problem in achieving economic growth in Ireland in the nineteenth century was the lack of risk capital rather than ordinary capital, which was apparently sufficient. It must be admitted, therefore, that the probability of the Church having diverted any considerable amount of risk capital to its own uses is not very great, and the argument that Irish economic growth was impeded by the Church's appropriation of a significant amount of capital is no longer viable.

The unviability, moreover, is reinforced by a reconsideration of a second basic assumption that I made in my article. I assumed that the Church was essentially a non-productive institution and that it was a drain on rather than a contributor to the Irish economy. In presenting the Church as a producer of services and not goods and in neglecting the Church's role as a consumer of both goods and services, I took too narrow a view. Some of the services produced by the Church, for example, and particularly in the area of education, certainly contributed in a positive way to the economy by improving skills and raising the literacy rate. In building an enormous plant in the course of the nineteenth century, moreover, the Church certainly increased the level of domestic demand, while a large portion of its income must have been spent in feeding and servicing the clerical population. Finally, I would now be prepared to admit that on balance the Church's role in the economy was more positive than I allowed twenty years ago, and may have indeed contributed to rather than retarded what improvement there was in the Irish economy. All of this, furthermore, has been given particular point by Liam Kennedy in a more recent article published in 1978.[2] Dr. Kennedy has ably argued to his and my satisfaction that the assumptions I made about the shortage of capital in Ireland and the Church being essentially a non-productive institution will not stand up in terms of the evidence now available.

While a great deal has been done, however, to improve our knowledge about Irish economic history in the last twenty years, literally nothing has been done, if Dr. Kennedy's article be excepted, about the economic role of the Church in Ireland in the nineteenth century. In spite of my obvious and stated reservations, therefore, I have decided to allow the article to be again reprinted almost as written. The heart of the article, as to how the Church built a formidable establishment in terms of plant and personnel in the course of the nineteenth century, is still, I believe, both sound and useful. The several appendices, moreover, are also of some value, especially as a starting point for some further estimate of Irish national income figures. Indeed, Dr. Kennedy and other scholars are generally agreed that my national income estimates are too low, and in the light of the evidence they have adduced at particular points in time, they are undoubtedly right.[3] Still, to date, no one has produced a more reliable set of national income figures, which must be the starting point for any meaningful estimate of Irish economic growth in the nineteenth century. The appendices may also prove useful as a starting point for a more detailed inquiry into what the Catholic community's share of that income was in the period under consideration. Given the sectarian nature of Irish politics and society, how far sectarianism affected the workings of the Irish economy and the distribution of wealth is a very important question, and may lead to some better understanding of to what extent there were different Protestant and Catholic economic life-styles as far as savings and investment and consumption patterns are concerned. I have decided, therefore, to allow the article to stand not only for what it says about the economic role of the Church, but also as a point of departure for further thinking about the implications of that role.

Though the second article in this volume, on the Devotional Revolution, has now been in print for more than ten years, I am happy to report that it has not only stood the test of time well, but it has become, in effect, the "new orthodoxy" in this area of Irish history.[4] If I were to revise it today, therefore, I would be more inclined to expand it than to change it. Indeed, the two articles that have been published on the subject since 1972 have done just that.[5] While accepting the fact of the Devotional Revolution, they have raised very pertinent questions about whether the cause that I assigned for this remarkable historical transformation was really the correct one. I argued that the reason why the Irish people became practicing Catholics as a people in the generation between 1850 and 1875 was that they had been suffering from a collective identity crisis caused by the gradual loss of the Irish language, culture, and way of life during the preceding century.

On the other hand, in his very interesting article published in 1975, Professor David Miller has argued that the real cause of the Devotional Revolution was the collapse of the whole peasant belief system, which constituted, in effect, an informal popular religion in pre-famine Ireland and which coexisted and competed with Roman Catholicism, the official and canonical belief system. The popular religion consisted of celebrations, magical observances and superstitions, which were intimately bound up with an agrarian cycle that reached its climax in the annual harvest. The collapse of this system was brought about by that awful social catastrophe, the

Great Famine, when the people's staple, the potato, succumbed to the blight in successive years between 1845 and 1848, destroying the credibility of the popular system and paving the way for the final triumph of the more formal and canonical system in the Devotional Revolution.

In a very persuasive article published in 1978, however, Eugene Hynes has taken both Miller and me to task for our explanation of the causes of the Devotional Revolution. Hynes argues that the crucial factor in making practicing Catholics of the Irish people in the nineteenth century was neither the collapse of the popular religion nor a collective identity crisis, but is rather to be found in a "great hunger" for land on the part of an Irish farmer elite, who were determined to maintain their standard of living in the face of adverse economic conditions both before and after the Famine and who found in the values and mores of the Devotional Revolution the religious canons that complemented their economic needs. This farmer elite, whose roots lay deep in the eighteenth century, found that after 1780 it was increasingly hardpressed by a rapidly increasing population to retain the amount of land necessary to maintain its basic standard of living. Through the stem family system, they adopted the necessary means, which included the control of capital by the head of the family, and the institution of a system of impartible inheritance in regard to the family farm, in order that the family should not sink into that myriad of cottiers and laborers at the bottom of a social pyramid that was expanding at so alarming a rate. Though the population began to decline rapidly after the Famine because of emigration and late marriage, the land hunger did not diminish among the former elite because larger farms were even more necessary in the shift from tillage to grazing enforced by long-term price trends for agricultural products, as well as the rising expectations of this elite class for a higher standard of living. "It is this great hunger," Hynes finally insists, "that explains both the initial acceptance and continued devotion to the Catholicism that became dominant in the nineteenth century."[6]

The important point to be made about all these explanations of the causes of the Devotional Revolution, of course, is that they are not mutually exclusive, and they may all be true to varying degrees. The real question, then, becomes which of the explanations is more credible in terms of the existing evidence and, therefore, more determinant perhaps than the others. Both Hynes and I posit a farmer-elite devotional nucleus, whose numbers relative to the cottier and laborer class were dramatically reversed by the Great Famine. We both, moreover, are emphatic about the need of this farmer elite for a Devotional Revolution, though we differ about what inspired that need. What prevented the Devotional Revolution from gaining more ground among the general population before the Famine was the adverse circumstances of population growth and the lack of money and personnel on the part of the Church. In a word, we both argue that before the Famine, the need was increasingly there, and most especially among a crucial class, but the Church did not have the resources to respond given the awful social circumstances.

In an important book published last year, however, Sean J. Connolly argued that the Devotional Revolution was essentially a post-Famine phenomenon and the impact of the formal Catholicism, that we have come to look upon today as the norm, was not much in evidence before 1845. Indeed, Dr. Connolly maintains:

> Throughout the decades before the Famine the religious practice of the great majority of Irish Catholics remained severely limited, in frequency of attendance, in the range of devotional observances, and in the degree of ceremony and external display with which public worship was conducted. By the end of this period, it is true, one can detect the beginnings of a movement for the imposition of new habits and standards, but this affected only a small minority.[7]

Given his thesis about the timing of the Devotional Revolution, Connolly naturally is not much concerned about why it took place. Still, he has raised at least two very important questions for those of us who have ventured to explain why the Devotional Revolution occurred, and especially for those of us who have argued that the need for it was there for a considerable time before the Famine. The first question has to do with the definition of the Devotional Revolution. Miller, Hynes, and I have taken weekly attendance at Mass as the main test of religious practice, while Connolly maintains that it also includes a whole "range of devotional observances" and their "degree of ceremony and external display." The second question raised by Connolly has really to do with the size and quality of the "minority" affected by the "new habits and standards" before the Famine.

I think it would now be generally agreed, by any definition, that the consolidation of the Devotional Revolution is a post-Famine achievement, the triumph of which may be dated symbolically from the National Synod of Maynooth in 1875, though some few areas and classes of people were not finally included until the 1880s. The real question, therefore, is no longer the "consolidation" of this phenomenon, but rather its "making," and this is really a question of when and how much of it was achieved before the Famine. On further reflection, I am inclined now to argue that a good deal more was achieved before the Famine than Connolly will allow, or that I was prepared to admit in my article. Miller has maintained, for example, that attendance at Mass in the 1830s for the whole of Ireland was in the range of forty percent. While the figure is low when compared to the ninety-five percent achieved in the fully consolidated Devotional Revolution, it is still a very substantial minority of the population and certainly cannot be characterized as "small." Moreover, as Miller points out, there is a substantial difference in attendance at Mass on an East-West axis, which is, in effect, to differentiate between an English- and an Irish-speaking Ireland. In the Eastern English-speaking rural areas, attendance at Mass may have been as high as seventy percent, while in the Western Irish-speaking rural areas it may have been as low as twenty. Though the quality of devotional practice was certainly not what it was to become after the Famine, the propensity for practice in English-speaking Ireland, and most especially in the towns, was very high. If to this is added the custom of stations in the rural areas described in my article, the devotional nucleus in terms of numbers at least must have been greater than that which Connolly is willing to allow. Finally, there is the question of how crucial was this farmer-elite in setting the example for the lesser farmers and even those lower down on the social scale.

If this farmer-elite, as I have maintained in the third article in this volume, was truly the nation-forming class, and that, if taken together with their cousinhood in the towns, they numbered more than 700,000 before the Famine, the argument made for their influence as well as their numbers is greater than I allowed for more than ten years ago. Why Connolly fails to appreciate the influence of this significant elite in pre-Famine Ireland is that he does not make enough allowance for either regional variations or class distinctions in his presentation. The popular religion of the Irish peasant, which he describes so well, was not only the belief system of those who still largely spoke Irish, but also of those who mainly found themselves at the bottom of the social pyramid. While they certainly made a majority of the Irish people before the

Famine, they can hardly be described as those who counted in terms of either power or influence in Irish society. Indeed, I do not think it would be outrageous to maintain, in spite of the considerable overlapping, that in pre-Famine Ireland, formal and canonical Roman Catholicism was the religious resort of the agricultural bourgeoisie, while the popular religion was largely the possession of the agricultural proletariat. So much, then, for what was achieved and by whom in the way of religious practice before the Famine. The question of when it was achieved, however, still remains. Connolly agrees that what was achieved was achieved very late, while Hynes would maintain that the crucial date was 1815, when the collapse of agricultural prices necessitated a shift from tillage to grazing, which intensified the "great hunger" for land by the farmer-elite. On the other hand, I would now be prepared to argue that this elite, which I have defined as the more than thirty-acre, tenant-farmer class, had been in existence from at least the middle of the eighteenth century and that it was this rural bourgeoisie that was the backbone of what constituted formal and practicing Catholicism before the rapid increase in population between 1800 and 1845 masked their importance as the devotional nucleus and crucial nation-forming class.

Besides expanding considerably, then, on the why, the how, and the when of the Devotional Revolution, I would also be tempted to treat at greater length the theme of the impact of the Devotional Revolution on the Irish abroad. Irish Catholicism became in the nineteenth century a world-wide phenomenon in the English-speaking world. Not only did the Roman Catholic Churches in England and Scotland become essentially Irish, but the Churches in the United States, English-speaking Canada, South Africa, Australia, and New Zealand were all strongly influenced by the developing values and mores of Irish Roman Catholicism. While the pastoral and administrative influence of Irish priests and bishops is easily made manifest in perusing the *Catholic Directories* of the various Churches in the English-speaking world, the missionary infrastructure that gave that hierarchical framework its breath of spiritual life has hardly been dealt with. What about the missions and the sermons, the retreats and the exhortations, the novenas and the devotions, the sodalities and the confraternities, the burial and temperance societies, the hospitals for the sick and the dying, the orphanages, the houses of refuge, and above all the school system on all levels? In what kinds of ways was this whole institutional structure permeated by the values, conscious and unconscious, of those who conducted it, and how did they adapt and modify those values in terms of their new environments? But whatever the answers to those questions turn out to be, the crucial factor will certainly be the cultural mind-set of those who had to make the decisions, and the mind-set that counted the most in the English-speaking world, as far as the Church was concerned, was Irish.

Finally, in thinking again about the third essay on "Church, State, and Nation" in this volume, I should merely like to repeat what I said in my previous introduction, because a number of critics of that article as originally published have not apparently read that introduction. I said then that if I were to add anything to this article I would perhaps say something more about the developing political consciousness of the Irish people in the late eighteenth century, which Daniel O'Connell was able to focus on with such great effect in his Catholic Association. I would now certainly point out that the crucial measure was the Catholic Relief Act of 1793, which gave Roman Catholics the vote and which in a generation resulted in an Irish electorate of more than 100,000. Before the Act of Union in 1800, which united Great Britain and Ireland, that developing Roman Catholic electorate made little difference because it was confined mainly to the county constituencies and was insignificant in the borough constituencies. When the Irish House of Commons, however, consisting of 64 county seats and 236 borough seats, or 300 in all, was reduced at the Union in 1800 to a representation of 100, consisting of the same 64 county seats but only 36 borough seats in the new Imperial Parliament, that redistribution of Irish seats made the Roman Catholic electorate in the counties real as far as actual political power was concerned. In effect, the British government made a large down-payment in the Act of Union on the substance of Catholic Emancipation, and when they did not fulfill their agreement, Daniel O'Connell effectively mobilized that down-payment to secure payment in full.

The Irish political system, therefore, was in the making for nearly a hundred years before it was finally consolidated by Parnell. This not only accounts, in part, for the remarkable stability of the system when it finally emerged, but it has some interesting implications for the political style of those millions of Irish who emigrated in the course of the nineteenth century. The important thing to remember, however, is that the values of the Irish political system were set very early by O'Connell. Mass politics was, in fact, created by him both in order to realize the power and to mask the poverty

and ignorance of his constituency. The level of political consciousness, therefore, of the Irish who emigrated was extraordinarily
high, especially if compared to other emigrant groups, and was
probably not exceeded by any other emigrant group except perhaps
the British. What made the Irish political style, however, appear
very sophisticated in its new environments was that the O'Connellite
mode not only involved mass organization, but a commitment to
the democracy and a real understanding of patronage politics.
When the Irish emigrated to the United States, therefore, they took
to Tammany Hall politics like the proverbial duck takes to water.
Just as a great deal more work, however, needs to be done on the
Irish abroad in terms of their ability to maintain their social identity,
the same is true with regard to their ability to project their political
power in the host societies. And just as the Irish emigrant was not
a social constant in terms of his values and behavior because of the
changing nature of the environment in Ireland in the course of the
nineteenth century, he was not a political constant either, and for
the same reasons. Understanding the Irish, either at home or
abroad, therefore, is not possible without first coming to terms with
the economic, social, and political context which formed them; and
it is hoped that these essays will contribute to that understanding.

Emmet Larkin
The University of Chicago
July 1983

NOTES

[1] Raymond D. Crotty, *Irish Agricultural Production* (Cork, 1966); L. M. Cullen, *An Economic History of Ireland since 1660* (London, 1972); Joseph Lee, *The Modernization of Irish Society, 1848–1918* (Dublin, 1973); Joseph Lee, "The Railways in the Irish Economy" and "Capital in the Irish Economy," in *Formation of the Irish Economy*, ed. L. M. Cullen (Cork, 1966).

[2] Liam Kennedy, "The Roman Catholic Church and Economic Growth in Nineteenth Century Ireland," *The Economic and Social Review*, October, 1978.

[3] Joseph Lee, "Irish Economic History since 1500," in *Irish Historiography, 1970–79*, ed. Joseph Lee (Cork, 1981), p. 177.

[4] M. A. G. O'Tuathaigh, "Ireland, 1800–1921," in *Irish Historiography, 1970–79*, ed. Joseph Lee (Cork, 1981), p. 102.

[5] David W. Miller, "Irish Catholicism and the Great Famine," *Journal of Social History*, September, 1975; Eugene Hynes, "The Great Hunger and Irish Catholicism," *Societas*, Spring, 1978.

[6] Hynes, p. 150.

[7] Sean J. Connolly, *Priests and People in Pre-Famine Ireland, 1780–1845* (Dublin, 1982), p. 98.

I

Economic Growth, Capital Investment, and the Roman Catholic Church in Nineteenth-Century Ireland

"Our poverty may appear contemptible, and even sordid," wrote Patrick Curtis, the archbishop of Armagh, to his agent in Rome in 1825, "but it is not really so." "We are, indeed, very poor, and I believe you know," he explained, dignifying the twenty pounds he enclosed for the rebuilding of St. Paul's Basilica in Rome, "that my Mitre, though Primatial, is one of the poorest in Ireland: and yet the claims on us are increasing. . . ."[1] Seventy-five years later, almost to the day, in 1900, his successor in the primatial see of Armagh, Michael Cardinal Logue, cleared over thirty thousand pounds in a single bazaar for the purpose of decorating the interior of his cathedral, and could afford to send regularly every year some six hundred pounds in Peter's pence to Rome.[2] What happened in those seventy-five years to account for this remarkable increase in the resources of the Church? This question might not prove nearly as interesting or even important, if Ireland, like Belgium, had experienced the full effects of an Industrial Revolution in the nineteenth century. Instead, by the turn of the century, well over five million people had fled the country, as Ireland remained one of the more economically backward areas in Western Europe. The anomaly, therefore, of a church that appeared to be growing ever more wealthy in a seemingly stagnant and chronically depressed economy raises a further question: what effect did the acquisition by the Church of a considerable amount of property over a relatively short period of time have on capital investment and economic growth in Ireland?

13

To begin to answer these questions it is first necessary to know something about the larger economic frame within which the Church itself existed. At the beginning of the nineteenth century, there were actually two economies in Ireland, one maritime and the other subsistence.[3] They are easily identifiable in that the former was based on money, and the latter was not. The real problem, however, is not in identifying these two economies, but in locating them. A straightforward geographical analysis will not do since it is not enough to point out that the relatively prosperous metropolises, like Dublin, Cork, and Limerick, and the lesser Irish ports, all with their available hinterlands, made up the maritime economy, while the mountains and bogs of Kerry and Connemara were typical of the subsistence economy. Actually, the subsistence economy permeated everywhere so that within each maritime area there was a subsistence sector. The relative size of this subsistence sector was an excellent indication of how healthy economically a maritime area really was.[4] The reason the Irish economy was so sick, and progressively growing more vulnerable before the Great Famine, was that the steady increase in population was continually enlarging the subsistence sectors within the maritime areas.[5]

These subsistence sectors were made up of a class of paupers, cottiers, and marginal farmers, who lived in hovels on their potato patches, paid their rent every year with a pig, and sold their labor or begged for those absolutely necessary amenities over and above their shelter and food. Anywhere from one-quarter to one-third of the people subsisted on this level, and as the population increased, they began to make up a terrifyingly larger proportion of the total. When the potato failed in 1846, this class was wiped out. In five years some two million people had either left the country or were dead of disease and hunger. Ironically enough, the effect of this awful catastrophe on the Irish economy was beneficial, for the subsistence economy was dealt a blow from which it never recovered, and within fifty years it was almost extinct. The countless number of potato patches, and the marginal farms of less than five acres, which had depended on the potato for their existence, were ruthlessly consolidated into economic holdings. The remaining congestion was further relieved by repeated failures of the potato crop in the early 1850's, the early 1860's, and the late 1870's. By the early 1880's therefore, that large class, which had made up the subsistence economy before the famine, had virtually been liquidated through emigration.[6]

The thirty years after the Great Famine, then, were among the most prosperous in Ireland's dismal economic history. The repeal of the corn laws in 1846 ushered in a golden age in British and Irish agriculture. The harvests, except for the potato, were bountiful year after year, and continued industrial expansion and population growth in Britain assured the Irish farmer of strong and steady prices for his products. With emigration hardening into a tradition, the Irish farmer also found the burden of providing for a poverty-stricken peasantry lighter every year, and his gradual shift from tillage to profitable grazing enabled him to meet the problem of a decreasing labor supply.[7] This almost idyllic situation came to an end in the late 1870's with the general collapse of British and Irish agriculture in the face of competition from the New World. A revolution in transport—railroads, refrigeration, and steamships—made it possible for American and Canadian grain, Argentine beef, Australian mutton, and New Zealand butter to undersell the local product in the home market.

The competition from the New World was made vivid by Thomas Nulty, bishop of the very wealthy diocese of Meath, in a letter to the rector of the Irish College in Rome. Nulty wrote on May 29, 1879:

> I never remember to have seen such a depression in trade and such universal poverty among the farming and grazing classes in this Diocese. We have scores of the most respectable farmers and graziers in this Diocese who have become bankrupt. Only think of plenty of the finest American beef for sale this moment in Mullingar! Probably I will dine on some of it today. Mullingar was famous for the superiority of its Beef and Mutton and only imagine these Americans underselling us even here.[8]

Tariff barriers were quickly erected in most European countries to protect the farmer, but in Britain, where free trade had almost become a religious truth, no such protection was forthcoming for fifty years. Three bad harvests in succession in the late 1870's marked the beginning of the end of Irish agricultural prosperity.[9] The agricultural depression deepened in the 1880's though there were partial recovery and some improvement between 1890 and 1914. But the prosperity of the mid-Victorian heyday was not to be experienced again, except for a brief interlude during the First World War, until more recent times.

This, then, was the general economic frame within which the Irish Church had to make its financial way in the nineteenth century. As the legal position of Catholics improved in the late eighteenth century, the Church had quietly begun to gather economic strength. By the turn of the century, however, the improvement in the Church's economic fortunes was still rather modest. In making his required report to Rome on the state of his diocese on November 29, 1802, John Young, bishop of Limerick, wrote that he had fifty-eight priests, ten of whom were regulars, for a population of about sixty thousand, which included some eight thousand Protestants.[10] In the city of Limerick, he added, there were four parish priests, fourteen curates, and nine regulars ministering to some five thousand families of which one thousand were Protestant. There were three schools for poor Catholics, which accommodated forty children and which the biship assured Rome were as good as the apostate school in his diocese. He also reported that he had twelve students in his seminary who studied logic, metaphysics, and theology. The confraternity established by his predecessor, the bishop noted, was doing well and was preventing the proselytizers from being as effective as they might. He then went on to report:

> 2. Besides the City, the Diocese of Limerick has five districts and some villages. In many of the rural Parishes there are two Chapels in both of which the Parish Priest celebrates Mass on Feast Days with Apostolic Indulgence for the comfort of the faithful who live there.

> 3. All the Chapels and Churches are well supplied with holy and precious furnishings, and especially that of the Mensal Parish of the Bishop, to which has been recently donated by one not of the faith a crystal candalabra of twelve lights of great value in thanks for having recovered his health.

> 4. After the loss of the National Colleges [on the Continent] a pious benefactor has given the Bishop a House for the founding, already under way, of a seminary in his Diocese for the Education of young men called to the Ecclesiastical state.[11]

This *relatio status* of the bishop of Limerick is important not only because there are fewer of them than one might expect during this period but because the diocese of Limerick was a limiting case. Limerick was a relatively wealthy maritime center with a reasonably prosperous Catholic merchant class, and if this modest statement in terms of property and personnel is one of the optimum cases, it is not difficult to imagine what the situation was in those dioceses less economically fortunate than Limerick.

Toward the other end of the spectrum was the *relatio*, dated November 23, 1804, of James Murphy, bishop of Clogher. After reporting at great length on the geography and places of religious interest in his diocese, as well as on the number, character, and learning of his clergy, Murphy wrote:

> Our illiterate laity, for nine tenths of our people owing to their great poverty are such, have made astonishing progress in acquiring a competent knowledge of the Christian Doctrine within a few years back. . . . I have to add to this that, in many Parishes; where not long ago we had the most wretched Cabbins of Chapels not half equal to contain the Congregation; and in others where there was no covering whatever for the People and scarcely a shed to shelter the Priest and Sacrifice; we have lately got many good Chapels erected and covered with the best of slate. We have at present six more nearly finished, and if God in his mercy is pleased to grant this Empire an honorable Peace shortly, I hope with his assistance and that of our Protestant Neighbors; for indeed they have been very kind to us on these occasions, we shall get Chapels round the whole Diocese in a few years.[12]

The main burden of meeting the Church's early capital needs, of course, fell on that class of laity who were relatively wealthy: the merchants and farmers who had made large sums of money during the wars of the French Revolution and the imperium by shipping foodstuffs to Britain and Wellington's army in the peninsula. On this economic well-being the Church was able to build a new, though modest, establishment where hardly any had existed before. The severe depression, which followed the end of the war in 1815, was a serious blow to Irish prosperity in general and to the agricultural sector, which was the mainstay of the Catholic middle classes, in particular. By 1825, however, there was a mild recovery, which continued until 1830, when the improvement was so rapid that the peak of the war years was nearly passed in the late 1830's. This upward trend, though modified in the early 1840's, continued until the shock of the Great Famine in 1846.[13]

The Church, of course, shared in the increase in wealth of its laity. In the half century before the famine, the cost of building and maintaining the Church establishment was about £30,000,000 or £600,000 per year on the average. Some £5,000,000 of this total, or £100,000 per year, went into capital improvements, mainly building, which included cathedrals, churches, chapels, convents, seminaries, schools, and housing for the clergy, while the larger part, £25,000,000, or £500,000 per year, went to support the clerical population. These calculations are based, in part, on an estimate made by the archbishop of Tuam, John MacHale, and the bishop of Ardagh, William Higgins, in 1847.[14] The estimate by these prelates of the Church's income in Ireland for the thirty years preceding 1847 was the result of a most violent division among the Irish bishops as to whether they should accept the Queen's colleges which were endowed by the state. In their ex parte statement to Rome condemning the state-endowed colleges as godless, MacHale and Higgins also argued that Ireland could afford to build its own system of Catholic higher education without state aid and adduced as their reason that the Church in Ireland over the previous thirty years had been able to raise a considerable sum for its own support and maintenance through the voluntary offerings of the faithful. In summing up, MacHale and Higgins presented the following breakdown of the major items in the budget of the Church between 1817 and 1847:

Building of Churches	£3,000,000
Parochial Houses	100,000
Convents for Nuns	240,000
Monasteries for Monks	200,000
Colleges	200,000
Schools for the Poor	200,000
Maintenance of the Clergy	18,000,000
Total	£21,940,000[15]

These figures are open to question, of course, because there is an obvious reason for MacHale and Higgins to be partisan in the presentation of their case to Rome. Their estimate with regard to the maintenance of the clergy, for example, is too high. The figure of £600,000 per year assumes that there were 4,000 priests in Ireland and each received on the average an income of £150 per year. While the income is plausible enough, the number of priests was closer to 2,500 than 4,000, and the yearly cost of maintaining the clergy was closer, therefore, to £400,000 than £600,000. Further, while the other estimates in the above list are all too high, however, no allowances are made for maintenance and upkeep of these establishments and for either the Catholic contribution to the expenses of the National System of Education, which was largely administered by the clergy, or for the system of schools established by the Irish Christian Brothers. When, therefore, what is left out is balanced against what is overestimated, MacHale's and Higgins' "statistics" are not as partisan as they might seem at first glance.

A most useful support and corrective for and to the above figures was presented in a thirty-four-page pamphlet published in Dublin in 1865. Major Myles O'Reilly, who had the confidence of nearly all the Irish bishops, maintained that:

> In twenty-five of the twenty-eight dioceses of Ireland, embracing 944 out of the 1,085 parishes into which Ireland is divided, there have been built in the sixty-three years since 1800:

1.	1805 Churches which have cost	£3,061,527*
2.	217 Convents which have cost	1,058,415
3.	40 Colleges or seminaries which have cost	308,918
4.	44 Hospitals, or Asylums, or Orphanages which have cost	147,135
	Making a total expenditure for these objects of	£4,575,995

> If the expenditure in the other one hundred and forty-one parishes was at the same rate it would make a total for Ireland of more than £5,274,368: but to this we may add the cost of erection of 2,990 National Schools erected without any Government aid, and under Catholic management. Now I have ascertained the cost of about four hundred schoolhouses in different parts of Ireland, and I find that the average is, £100; the cost of these 2,990 schools will, therefore, amount to £299,000, which, added to the foregoing, makes £5,573,368. Yet, even thus, we are far from having a complete estimate of the amount expended by the Catholics of Ireland in buildings for religious, charitable, and educational purposes during the century. We have taken no note of the many schools, such as those of the Christian Brothers,** and others not in connection with the National Board; we have not included the cost of parochial houses for the clergy with which, perhaps, about one-third of the parishes in Ireland are provided. All these and many other heads I would have wished to include in these returns, but it would have been impossible to have given them with accuracy.

* In very few instances have the value of materials and labour given been included; consequently this item is considerably understated. It is also to be observed that in several instances a church was built soon after 1800, which has since been pulled down and another handsomer substituted; thus, in the Parish of Askeaton, Diocese of Limerick, two thatched churches were built in 1804, about 1850 they were replaced by two handsome stone ones which cost £3,700. In these cases only the cost of the last erections is given.

** The sixty-eight schools of the Christian Brothers alone must cost at least £68,000.[16]

Most of this income was contributed in dues by the laity in money and kind at Christmas and Easter, and from offerings at baptisms, marriages, and funerals, as well as for dispensations and the saying of Masses. The larger sums came in the form of gifts, subscriptions, and special collections; as Catholic wealth accumulated, the number of charitable and pious bequests also increased. This increase in clerical income was graphically described by a Carlow priest, James Maher, in the early 1840's in a letter to his nephew, Paul, later Cardinal, Cullen, who was then the rector of the Irish College in Rome.

> In travelling thru the Country I have observed with pain that the relative position of the people and Clergy has been greatly changed. The people have become very much poorer. And the Clergy have adopted a more expensive style of living. The best Catholic house in each Parish and the best style of living appears to be the Priests. Time was when both parties were more upon an equality. The demands of the Priests on the People have greatly multiplied and the laity are beginning to complain. Dues, dues is the perpetual cry, the constant Sundays theme of some. The Alter is occupied for an hour every Sunday, for the transactions of the Priests and oats and turf, and all the arrears of Baptisms and unctions. What a desecration! . . . The people of some parts of Connaught, have combined to resist the payment of dues to the Priest, unless according to a scale which they themselves devised. This is a bad sign of the times. The movement however at present is nearly hushed, but I fear it will again break out.[17]

With the approach of the famine, then, the Church actually appeared to be getting poorer and poorer, while its clergy were getting richer and richer. The reason for this strange variation on a Marxian theme was the rapid rise in population. While clerical incomes naturally increased as births, deaths, and marriages increased, there was at the same time a consequent need to expand the Church establishment to minister to this increased population, but the capital necessary for this expansion was not available. The best example of the Church's capital needs not being met before and during the famine are the statistics relating to the "Sums Expended on the Erection and Repairs of Buildings at Maynooth College" between 1796 and 1852.[18] Maynooth had been established by an act of Parliament in 1795 to provide for the education of priests for the Roman Catholic Church in Ireland. A grant of £8,000 was then made, later increased to £9,000 per year, and in 1845 increased to £26,000 per year to support faculty, administration, and 500 free places for seminarians. From time to time provisions were also made by Parliament for the cost of building and repairs, but mainly Maynooth was expected to rely on the subscriptions of Catholics for new building and repairs. In 1807 Parliament voted £5,000 for new buildings and in 1845 again voted £30,000, while between 1846 and 1852 it voted some additional £7,000 for repairs. Significantly, between 1836 and 1845, absolutely nothing was spent on new buildings at Maynooth, and the decreasing sums spent on repairs between 1840 and 1843 become even more interesting when they are related to the three successive bad harvests in the early 1840's because they relfect the dependence of the Church on the farming and merchant classes for supplying its capital needs. By the early 1840's then, the Church was actually income rich and capital poor because the class that had been meeting the capital needs of the Church was itself financially embarrassed.

The Catholic merchants and farmers also seem to have been regularly investing the largest part of their surplus capital in land, which improvident Irish landlords were mortgaging to the maximum, thus reducing their ready supply of money. In the summer of 1835 Alexis de Tocqueville, who was touring Ireland, asked William Kinsella, bishop of Ossory, for example, "Is it true that the Protestant aristocracy is very much in debt?" Kinsella replied:

> Yes. Nothing is more true. Most of them give way under the burden of their commitments. Every day we see the rich Catholics of the towns lend money to Protestants, and the latter are finally obliged to break the "entail" and to sell their land. In this way much land gradually falls into the hands of the Catholics. Recently in this county two Catholics, Mr. X and Mr. Y, bought land, the one for £20,000 and the other for £30,000,[19]

A few days after this interview with the bishop of Ossory in Kilkenny, and on his way to Cork, Tocqueville again noted:

> At Mitchelstown there is a spendid mansion belonging to Lord Kingstown. He has 75,000 acres round the house. He lives there. I was shown a huge clearing which he has had made, and which is covered with fine crops; and a row of clean and convenient cottages which he has had built for his tenants. It is said that he has made money out of doing this. The town of Mitchelstown does not look as wretched as the rest of the country.

> I ask where the "Lord" is. I am told that he went off his head two years ago. Why? I am told that it is because he found himself burdened

SUMS EXPENDED ON THE ERECTION AND REPAIRS OF BUILDINGS AT MAYNOOTH COLLEGE
from its establishment in 1795, to January 1st, 1852

Year	New Buildings			Repairs			Year	New Buildings			Repairs		
	£	s.	d.	£	s.	d.		£	s.	d.	£	s.	d.
1796		—		89	3	1	1829		—		256	17	6
1797	5,524	2	2	67	17	8	1830		—		453	15	1½
1798	4,000	0	0	32	12	10½	1831	5,842	4	0	251	7	0
1799	3,869	15	3	65	18	6	1832	452	16	8	229	12	3½
1800	4,827	8	7½	51	3	8½	1833	6,573	13	10	242	13	1
1801	1,806	16	7½	62	13	7	1834	380	7	0	341	19	8½
1802				77	7	2	1835	1,527	13	8	354	19	7½
1803	541	12	6	248	16	0	1836	1,176	3	8	515	0	5½
1804		—		778	16	4	1837		—		499	3	8½
1805		—		728	4	4½	1838		—		400	15	4
1806	2,469	19	10	114	3	5½	1839		—		291	12	8
1807	2,530	0	2	76	2	4	1840		—		340	16	0½
1808	6,241	10	5½	280	16	11½	1841		—		269	9	4
1809				189	6	8	1842		—		206	6	10

Year	£	s	d	£	s	d
1810				161	19	11½
1811	121	2	8	533	3	1½
1812				796	4	5½
1813				218	1	1
1814				206	18	5
1815				252	14	1½
1816	4,043	10	0	454	12	0
1817				288	2	8
1818				511	3	10½
1819				163	8	10½
1820				285	12	3
1821	100		0	443	18	9
1822				597	1	3½
1823				319	5	0½
1824	6,500	0	0	301	18	3½
1825				254	10	4½
1826	1,351	7	7½	226	18	0
1827	1,120	10	4	261	17	8½
1828				252	6	4

Year	£	s	d
1843	189	18	10
1844	311	12	7½
1845	308	12	10½
1846	1,189	7	10
1847	1,047	3	4½
1848	1,540	3	2
1849	1,292	7	10½
1850	1,129	10	9½
1851	1,009	9	4½
	30,737	17	5
	—	—	

with £400,000 of debts without hope of ever being able to pay them off. The money had been lent him by Catholic merchants in Cork on mortgage of the huge estates which I had seen, and absorbed almost all his income. It is like that almost every where in Ireland. Witness the finger of God. The Irish Aristocracy wanted to remain separated from the people and be still English. It has driven itself into imitating the English Aristocracy without possessing either its skill or its re-sources, and its own sin is proving its ruin. The Irish were turned out of their lands by force of arms. Hard work is bringing them back again into these estates.[20]

The burden on this Catholic middle class by the 1840's, however, was growing intolerable, for every year they had to face an increase in the number of the poor and meet the rising cost of the agitation for repeal, as well as the mounting capital needs of the Church. All this occurred, moreover, when they themselves were greatly reduced in circumstances by three successive bad harvests. Maher wrote Cullin in Rome:

> The labouring classes were never so poor, or so unemployed as in the present year. The farmers by a succession of bad harvests have been drained to the last penny and can give no employment. The potato crop has been most defective; and things now would be at famine price but for Peel's Corn Law Bill, and Foreign Cattle Bill; the people are emigrating in great numbers. Even those who have some means in their hands, are going, and others of the same class are speaking of following them.[21]

In the early 1840's, therefore, the Church was forced to consider other courses than its impoverished middle classes, if it were not to be financially swamped.

After its laity, however, it could go only to the banks and the British government. Credit without collateral, whether the bank was Protestant or Catholic, was not easily obtained. The British government, on the other hand, for political reasons, was a some-what less reluctant source. Parliament passed a Charitable Bequests Act, which better secured property bequeathed to the Church, and thereby strengthented its credit position. It also voted £30,000 to the seminary at Maynooth to provide for necessary capital improve-ments and nearly tripled the annual grant of £9,000 to that institution. Some of the capital strain on the Church was also relieved when an increasing number of the clergy began to plow large sums, which they had saved out of their clerical earnings, back into the Church establishment. Maher bitterly wrote his nephew:

Father Kearney's clerical savings (about £10,000, some say £12,000) although bequeathed to charitable purposes have given little edification: how did [he] scrape together and hoard up everyone asks, such as enormous sum? Legacy duty (it is now 10 percent when property is bequeathed to those who are not next of kin) will be £1000. What a waste! It could have been avoided by a transfer of the property to trustees upon a pound stamp. . . . Besides Kearney's £10,000 the Church has had another windfall in the Death of the Revd Nicholas Sharman of Kilkenny. He left £3,000 to charitable purposes, the poor of his parish, and £500 to a sister. He had had some private property, and nobody therefore censures the bequest to his sister. . . . Another rich priest (Tracy) died in Ossory a year or two since, intestate, leaving a large sum, several thousands, to be scrambled for, by his next of kin: you have heard already of the £1500 which the late Parish Priest of Allen (Dunne) died possessed of, and of the £1000 which the niece of Father O'Rourke of Celbridge relieved him of. I had nearly forgotten old Prendergast's £6,000. What do you think of this merchandize in the Church: All the cases I have mentioned, are of recent occurrences, and within a very circumscribed circle. The economy of these money savers in the midst of a poor people has damaged the character of the clergy exceedingly.[22]

Still, this combination of what the Church could politely borrow from the banks, genteelly beg from the British government, and informally levy from its clergy was not nearly enough to meets its capital needs.

Then suddenly and dramatically the whole situation was changed by the Great Famine, and the Church, which has been straining at every financial nerve for nearly a decade, now found itself growing stronger instead of weaker every year. The reason for this startling change, of course, was that the Catholic merchants and farmers had partially come into their own again. The landed estates, in which they had been investing heavily before the famine, were put up for sale in the Encumbered Estates Court. They proceeded to buy out these mortgaged estates as freeholders and were no longer merely the renters, but the owners, of the means of production.[23] The really important point, however, is that the Catholic population had substantially increased its share of the national income.

The Church almost instinctively started to gear its administrative apparatus to the new and more favorable economic situation. At the National Synod of Thurles in 1850, the Church began to rationalize its own economic position. Measures were enacted, for example, to make it more likely that clerical savings would be plowed back into the establishment rather than be dissipated among numerous relatives.[24] The title to ecclesiastical property, furthermore, was to be vested in trustees, of whom the bishop was to be one, to prevent it from falling into the personal estate of deceased clergymen. In order to channel the entrepreneurial activities and talents of priests into ecclesiastical rather than secular pursuits, restrictions were also placed on the priests owning or farming land, though many continued to do so in the names of their brothers and nephews.[25] Twenty-five years later, in 1875, the statutes approved at Thurles were strengthened and reinforced at the Synod of Maynooth.[26] The statutory improvements at Thurles, meanwhile, were invigorated by a gradual reform in the Irish episcopacy. A greater emphasis in episcopal appointments after 1850 was laid on administrative talents and business capacity. Most of the new bishops had received their administrative training as presidents and rectors of seminaries and colleges, and this proved to be an excellent apprenticeship for the men who eventually would have to undertake the more complex problem of managing a diocese.

The lead given by this new generation of bishops had an almost contagious effect on their priests; nowhere was this more evident than in the ambitious building programs undertaken by the clergy, high and low, between 1850 and 1880. "There is still a great deal of poverty in the Country," Michael Kiernan, archbishop of Armagh, wrote Tobias Kirby, rector of the Irish College in Rome, "but the condition of the people is on the whole improving, and there is hardly a Diocese in Ireland in which there are not two or three magnificent Churches in the course of erection, not to speak of convents, schools which are rapidly spreading in every direction over the land."[27] The most ambitious building project undertaken by the Church in nineteenth-century Ireland was undoubtedly the cathedral at Queenstown, now Cobh. It was begun in 1868 in a most optimistic and enthusiastic spirit. "The priests and people," wrote William Keane, bishop of Cloyne, to Kirby, "have taken up the collection in the most cheerful and generous manner; Mistleton Parish giving 450£; Cloyne 250£; Aghada 230£ & &. Nearly a hundred men have been at work at the building for eight or nine months past. It is pleasant to see the walls rising up."[28] Some ten years later, John McCarthy, Keane's successor in the see of Cloyne, reported that the cathedral had already cost £65,000 and £20,000 more would be necessary before Mass could be said in it. "It was commenced," he complained, "on too magnificent and costly a scale for the resources of the Diocese, but it was so far advanced when it fell into my hands that I could make no change without spoiling it."[29] "I have got," McCarthy then added, "nearly £3,000 from the priests I sent to Australia. I am now thinking of sending out two more to America to collect." More than thirty years later, in 1910, McCarthy's successor, Robert Browne, was still complaining about the cathedral to another rector of the Irish College.[30] He noted that since the foundation stone had been laid, the cathedral had cost £150,000 and was still £3,000 in debt. He lamented, moreover, that the end was not in sight because the cathedral still lacked a tower and spire. His people were financially exhausted, and he did not know where to turn because collections had been taken up in America three times and in Australia once.

Meanwhile cathedrals, churches, chapels, convents, monasteries, seminaries, parochial houses, episcopal palaces, schools, colleges, orphanages, hospitals, and asylums all mushroomed in every part of Ireland. This energy was supplemented by an ingenuity, a perseverance, and a confidence that would make the most hard-headed exponent of the Protestant ethic gasp. Bazaars, pilgrimages, shrines, altar societies, sodalities, confraternities, special collections on almost every Sunday and holiday of the year, and clergy collecting and canvassing the far-flung Irish missionary empire became an integral part of the Irish Catholic way of life. Fortunately for the Church, this revolution in church building was largely complete by the time the agricultural depression hit Ireland in the late 1870's, and the period between 1880 and 1914 was mainly devoted to consolidation. The financial apparatus and techniques, however, developed to meet the costs of building were not greatly impaired by the depression, and, in fact, as Catholics' share of the national income declined, the Church's share of it appeared to increase.

One unmistakable sign of the continued and developing prosperity of the Church between 1850 and 1900 was the impressive increase in the clerical population. In 1850 there were about 5,000 priests, monks, and nuns for a Catholic population of 5,000,000, while in 1900 there were over 14,000 priests, monks, and nuns for some 3,300,000 Catholics, or a ratio increase from 1 : 1000 in 1850 to 1 : 235 in 1900.[31] These figures become even more impressive when it is understood that the Church continued to export a large number of clerics at an increasing rate over this whole period.[32] By 1900 the Church had also a long tradition of exporting capital as well as clergy. Since 1860, when Peter's pence was inaugurated in Ireland with a contribution of £80,000, the Church had been able to sustain a yearly contribution of about £10,000 to Rome.[33] The

Irish Church, moreover, had been making sizable annual contributions to the Society for the Propagation of the Faith in Lyons since 1840.[34] These exports in capital and in personnel are one more indication of the Irish Church's capacity to mobilize capital and personnel during this period without apparently overtaxing its own resources.

An even surer barometer, perhaps, of the Church's developing economic strength was the increasing ease with which it could borrow money from the banks. Its credit position had so improved by 1900 that bishops were very often obliged to interfere with imprudent priests and nuns who had borrowed too heavily for ecclesiastical purposes.[35] The main source of all this new-found wealth was the increasing number and amount of gifts and bequests left to the Church for religious and charitable purposes.[36] After 1850 an ever-increasing part of the Church's income in Ireland was derived from legacies and bequests. The sharp competition for legacies and bequests that developed between the clergy and the relatives of the pious benefactors not only illustrated the above trend in Church income but also introduced some interesting moral and social tensions. Patrick Leahy, archbishop of Cashel, for example, wrote Kirby on November 15, 1864:

> Another matter is most urgent and you must get it settled for me at once. A Parish Priest of this Diocese died some time ago, leaving about £10,000, two thirds to establish a Convent of Sisters of Mercy, in his Parish, one third to establish Christian Brothers. He made this large sum chiefly by a judicious management of a little property, and then when he realised something by a judicious investment of it. He had an immense number of relatives, all needy, but left them only £200 cash, three nephews, £100 a niece, and provided for another niece in a Convent. He was under many obligations to one brother of his, yet left nothing to his Family. Now, I think it but comfortable to natural justice to give something more to his Family, say £500, and I have intimated to them that I w^d get this done. Moreover, if not done the Family may go to law, in which case the whole £10,000 may be lost when you consider how prejudiced the tribunals are against Catholic Charities. If not lost, at any rate more than £500 w^d be lost in expenses. So, it is best to give away to the Relations this sum. Quite enough remains to establish the Convent and Monastery. Get the Holy Father to give me power to dispose of £500 of the Legacy of Revd Patrick Hickey, P. P. of Doone. He was very averse, but unseasonably, to give any more to his Family.[37]

Some thirty years later a curate in the county Tyrone wrote Kirby's successor in the Irish College, enclosing £100 for the Propagation of the Faith in Africa and Asia from a parishioner. "He gave it to me," the young priest explained, "privately with a request, that his relations should not hear of his act." "I think I may add," he concluded discreetly, "that he has made a provision in his will for a large sum to go to the Propagation of the Faith, but this is not to be made known as long as he is alive."[38]

By 1905 there was not only sharp competition for legacies between the Church and the families of the benefactors but also among the various orders and institutions within the Church itself. The following series of letters from the bishop of Down and Connor, Henry Henry, to Michael O'Riordan, rector of the Irish College in Rome, between 1906 and 1908, is a good indication of how keen the competition had become. Henry wrote O'Riordan from Belfast:

I am anxious to obtain from the Holy Father himself a favour on behalf of two ladies, whose names are Hannah Hamill and Teresa Hamill French House, Belfast. These two ladies are the only survivors of a family of seven. About four years ago their brother Arthur died leaving me a bequest of a £1000 for my personal use and all his property, which is calculated to be worth £100,000 to his six sisters, four of them are since dead having made no disposition of their share of this vast estate so that it is entirely at the disposal of Hannah and Teresa. They hinted to me that they thought they should settle their affairs at once. With this I agreed and one of them said that as they had no relatives needing anything they should give all to God for the good of their souls. How they are to do this is still undecided, but I think I might be able to advise them rightly if I can keep in their Grace. They are, however, very changeable. They feel very lonely after so many deaths and believe that they will not live long, the youngest being over sixty. They asked me to get for them from the Pope, the right of receiving the Blessed Sacrament in their Oratory. I got the privilege of an Oratory for them from Propaganda during Arthur's life-time. They said they would not be so lonely if they could go to speak to our Lord. I undertook to do my best to get them this great privilege, telling them at the same time that I had been refused in another case, with which they are acquainted. Propaganda refused to renew the privilege granted for 3 years by the late Prefect in favour of Mr. Caffrey. In the end he got it through a Passionist Father from the Pope himself. The Passionist, however, had a letter from me which he presented to the Holy Father. Now I am satisfied if you presented my petition to the Holy Father he would grant it in this case. I fear it would be useless to ask at Propaganda. These ladies are very good and pious but are descended from Protestant blood. They have great reverence for the new Pope as they call him. They read a great deal about him—and like him. I need not say how pleased I would be to get the privilege for them.[39]

Less than a month later Henry wrote O'Riordan again, obviously pleased:

> Your letter enclosing the document with the Pope's autograph—graciously granting our petition in favour Misses' Hamill came to hand all right. I have not yet had time to go out to see them on the matter. I have scored out the last sentence of the second reason, but I think it will be better to let them know that one of the reasons, which influenced His Holiness to grant them the great privilege of having the Blessed Sacrament in their house was the fact that they were likely to give their property for pious uses. Unfortunately they are being besieged by the heads of religious orders male and female, from Dublin and even England and Scotland, as well as by priests from the Diocese. The most of their *Bona* consists of lands & houses in the neighbourhood of the city. It is being dinned into their ears that the Bishop has more than he needs even for charitable purposes. I am endeavouring to induce them to leave to me and trustees for Catholic charitable purposes in the Diocese their lands and houses after death. So far I have not succeeded. Of course if I succeeded your suggestion could be entertained. I need not approach them on the subject at present.[40]

"You remember the old ladies named Hamill," Henry wrote O'Riordan nearly a year later, "for whom you got a great privilege sometime ago." "Designing and envious clerics and even nuns," he complained bitterly, "have succeeded in alienating them from me, telling them that I have too much money." "I understand," he then concluded, "that they have settled their affairs not at all satisfactory in the interests of religion."[41] Several weeks later Henry again wrote O'Riordan on the subject of the sisters Hamill:

> I think I am bound to remove from your mind the impression made by my last letter regarding the manner in which the Misses Hamill are said to have disposed of their money. I thought I had them convinced of the propriety of making me a Trustee of their property and giving me discretionary power in reference to the manner of expending it for the advancement of religion. Some priests and nuns got around them and persuaded them that I had the handling of too much money. They induced them to exclude me from being a Trustee and gave away most of the property to charities, which are in a sense not charitable as they have at present, as I only know, abundant means for the objects of their institutes. My intention was to establish new centers of charitable works such as the Hospice for the Dying, free places for the higher education of our church and lay students, crèches for the poor children of the workers.
>
> As far as I have been able to find out they have left all or nearly all to what they have been told are charitable objects. I hope I have made myself clear this time. They may of course change their minds.[42]

The bishops, especially after 1890, with the most expensive days of the building revolution over, and the worst of the agricultural depression past, found they had much more surplus capital available. They invested this money, naturally enough, very conservatively in government securities, railway debentures, and first mortgages on land. The advice, for example, given by Michael Cardinal Logue, archbishop of Armagh, to Michael Kelly, rector of the Irish College in Rome, when the latter asked the former about investing some of the college funds in Ireland, told much about the investment policies of the Church in Ireland.

> You have hit on a very unfortunate time for your investment. Trustee securities are so high now that you can find none which will pay more than 2½ or 2¾ per cent. A few days ago I sold out near five thousand pounds of Government Stock which was left me for a charity, and I had just to put it in the Bank to wait for some investment. I think your best plan is to do the same for a time; but you should insist on the National Bank giving you a special rate for it. The only trustee security now that will give as much as four per cent is first mortgage on land; but it is not every mortgage one can trust. I intend to look out for such a mortgage to invest my charity money. Mr. [James] McCann says that if it could be got in a good County, such as Wexford, Kildare or Meath, with a good margin of Rental, it is quite safe. If trade improves securities will go down, and then there will be some chance of investing.[43]

While the bishops thus reduced the amount of risk capital available in the economy, they were finally able, with a steady income, to meet their fixed obligations without recourse to borrowing and eventually to wipe out their debts. By 1914 the Irish Church faced the financial future with a serenity and an optimism, that could only be matched in Ireland by Arthur Guinness and Sons Limited.

How the Church acquired its property in the nineteenth century is a relatively simple question to answer compared to the problem of what effect the increase in wealth had on capital investment and economic growth in Ireland. The main difficulty is that there are no separate national income figures for Ireland; they must be estimated on the basis of a crude extrapolation from British figures.[44] While these Irish figures appear credible enough in the light of what is known, they are not yet, of course, without the empirical corrective that only extensive research can produce, the kind of stuff out of which confident generalizations, let alone history, can be made. Still, to paraphrase an Irish revolutionary: somehow, somewhere, and by someone a beginning must be made.

Between 1801 and 1901, therefore, Irish national income only increased from £35,000,000 per year to £82,000,000 per year, while British national income grew over the same period from £232,000,000 to £1,643,000,000. This estimate of Irish national income, however, immediately poses a number of other awkward problems. What, for example, was the Catholic share of Irish national income, since most property in Ireland was in Protestant hands? Further, did the Catholic share tend to increase, diminish, or remain constant over the course of the century? Finally, how much of that Catholic income was available for capital investment and economic growth? The Catholic share probably did not amount to more than half the total Irish national income. There is no doubt Irish Catholics increased their share of national wealth in the nineteenth century, but since there are no statistics it is difficult to say by how much. If education level and occupations are any real indication of the distribution of wealth, the comparative statistics from the census of 1861 are at least instructive if not conclusive.

In 1800 the Catholics who, in Ireland, were "employed in literature and education," were a mere handful; in 1861 we find the number to be 23,180 Catholics and 17,660 Protestants of all sects; "employed in science and art" 359 Catholics, 398 Protestants. In 1800 the Catholics (who had obtained the privilege of belonging to the Learned professions only seven years before) hardly numbered any members of those professions amongst their ranks. In 1861 the numbers were, Catholics 4,875; Protestants, 6,820.* Taking altogether those classes which may be considered as engaged in occupations which require superior mental cultivation, we find the numbers to be, Catholics, 61,023; Protestants, 58,552**

*	Catholics	Protestants
Clergymen, 48 per cent.	3,014	3,264
Barristers, 28 " "	216	542
Attorneys, 35 " "	674	1,208
Physicians & Surgeons, 32 per cent.	761	1,597
Apothecaries, 50 per cent.	210	209
(Other liberal professions) engineers, architects, etc. 33 per cent.	358	718

**	Catholics	Protestants
Literature and Education	23,180	17,660
Justice and Government	25,541	23,542
Banking and Agency	1,820	2,735

Religion	6,251	4,374
Charity	514	468
Science and Art	359	398
Health	3,358	3,375[45]

The Catholic share of national income, moreover, did not appear to increase relative to the Protestant over the course of the century. The difficulty of relating wealth to landownershipo has already been noticed, but wealth is also reflected by political power, and even more so, perhaps, by administrative power. The general tendency toward the widening of the franchise in Britain and Ireland in the nineteenth century, naturally, weakened the relationship between the ownership of property and political power. This, however, was a much slower process in Ireland than in Britain, and before the 1880's parliamentary representation told more about the relationship than after. In 1861 there were 32 Catholic M.P.'s in an Irish representation of 103. Catholics also increased their administrative power in the nineteenth century, but rather more slowly than even the increase in their political power, and interestingly enough it seemed to increase more rapidly in the higher echelons than in the lower. Myles O'Reilly noticed that by 1861

Ireland, like England, has twelve judges of the superior courts: of these twelve eight are Catholics; of all the judges 33 per cent are Catholics; of course, I need hardly say that in 1800 there was not one. In England and Ireland justices of the peace are landed proprietors who are unpaid magistrates—the number of Catholics amongst them is, therefore, a good test of their social position. Of all the magistrates in Ireland 24 per cent are Catholics; of those who in the census are returned as "Ladies and Gentlemen" 27 per cent are Catholics; of bankers and agents, and merchants, 40 per cent are Catholics.[46]

By 1861, therefore, Catholics in Ireland, it would appear, did not own half the wealth. It is also apparent they were increasing their share of it slowly over the course of the century, and the claim that they acquired half is truer as one approaches 1900 than as one leaves 1800. It now becomes clearer that Irish nationalism was rooted in something more tangible than Irish Catholics' being "conscious" of their being merely Irish. They were also aware they were economically, culturally, socially, and politically deprived.

Before the famine, the propertied classes—landlords, manufacturers, industrialists, professional men, and government employees—were nearly all Protestant. Though Catholics increased their share in the agricultural sector after the famine by buying out Protestant landlords, this was more than balanced by the increased rate of growth in the industrial sector after 1850 in Protestant Ulster.[47] By 1880, in fact, with the agricultural sector in sharp decline, what increase there was in Irish national income was almost entirely attributable to the continued growth of the manufacturing and industrial sectors which were almost all owned by Protestants. On the other hand, there was some compensation on the Catholic side as they steadily increased their share of professional and governmental posts. The staying power of the Protestant ascendancy, however, was remarkable. The distribution of places and rewards, for example, on the Local Government Board, a public body founded in 1898, was the subject of some bitter criticism by Catholics in 1901.[48] In both the appointive and competitive categories on the board, Catholics maintained they were discriminated against. They also complained that Protestants were consistently better rewarded than Catholics for the same categories of work. As might be suspected, the dominance of Protestant influence was even more marked on the private area than in the public.[49]

If it is assumed, then, that the Catholic share of Irish national income was not more than half, and that it remained relatively constant over the century, how much of it was available for capital investment? The sad answer is comparatively little. Annual per capita income figures for Catholics in Ireland reveal that the margin, over and above what was absolutely necessary for subsistence in a money economy, was extremely narrow, and especially so before the famine.[50] A rough estimate of what was available for all purposes over and above subsistence averages out to a little less than £3,000,000 per year before 1850 and £7,000,000 per year after 1850.[51] What then was the Church's share? Before the famine the Church had some £600,000 of the £3,000,000 available, or some 20 per cent, while after the famine, the Church's share was not less than £1,000,000 of the £7,000,000 available, or nearly 15 per cent.[52]

Did this appropriation, then, by the Church of so large a share of what was available over and above subsistence inhibit economic growth? Before the famine it probably did not make much difference what the Church appropriated to itself. For even if the Catholic middle classes had managed to save for more productive purposes what they invested in land, contributed to the Church, and gave to support the political agitation, as well as cut consumption to the bone, it would not have been enough to sustain a shift from an agricultural to an industrial base given the increase in population. Without substantial external aid, therefore, the economic situation in Ireland simply bordered on the hopeless. After the famine the situation improved to the extent at least that the possibility, if not the probability, of growth existed. The Church, by building and maintaining a large organization devoted to producing services rather than goods, and consuming some 3 per cent of the Catholic share of national income and nearly 15 per cent of what was available over subsistence, certainly increased the probabilities against economic growth.

The question of the Church's impeding economic growth in Ireland, of course, does not end simply with an account of how much capital it was able to divert to its own needs. The Church, for example, not only absorbed capital, but also entrepreneurial talent, and why no risk takers emerged in Catholic Ireland is almost as important a question as why there was so little risk capital available. If the Church, then, had such a serious effect on these economic determinants of growth, what, indeed, must have been its impact on the social determinants of growth? What effect, for example, did exclusive and sectarian policies in marriage and education, as well as clerical celibacy, devotional piety, and other life orientation have on values, family, class structure, social cohesion, and individualism? A consideration of these problems now would only turn this attempt at a conclusion into another paper. The responsibility for impeding Irish economic growth in the nineteenth century, however, extends beyond even the Church to the British government in Ireland and the Catholic middle classes. The problem of the British government in Ireland has been resolved in this century by nationalism and the creation of a Free State. The Catholic middle classes, further, have been made aware of their economic responsibilities by a strong dose of unacknowledged Socialism and the creation of a welfare state. Only the Church in Ireland has escaped the heavy hand of the general will in the twentieth century.

APPENDIX A

The statistics with regard to emigration (1), evictions (2), and consolidation of holdings (3) after the famine are conclusive in proving that this subsistence class was liquidated.

1. Emigration:

Year	Total Number of Overseas Emigrants from Ireland	Number Emigrating to United States	Year	Total Number of Overseas Emigrants from Ireland	Number Emigrating to United States
1845	74,970	50,207	1873	83,692	75,536
1846	105,917	68,023	1874	60,496	48,136
1847	219,885	118,120	1875	41,449	31,433
1848	181,316	151,003	1876	25,976	16,432
1849	218,842	180,189	1877	22,831	13,991
1850	213,649	184,351	1878	29,492	18,602
1851	254,537	219,232	1879	41,296	30,058
1852	224,997	195,801	1880	93,641	83,018
1853	192,609	156,970	1881	76,200	67,339
1854	150,209	111,095	1882	84,132	68,300
1855	78,854	57,164	1883	105,743	82,849
1856	71,724	58,777	1884	72,566	59,204

Year			Year		
1857	86,233	66,080	1885	60,017	50,657
1858	43,281	31,498	1886	61,276	52,858
1859	52,981	41,180	1887	78,901	69,084
1860	60,835	52,103	1888	73,233	66,306
1861	36,322	28,209	1889	64,923	57,897
1862	49,680	33,521	1890	57,484	52,110
1863	116,391	94,477	1891	58,436	53,438
1864	115,428	94,368	1892	52,902	48,966
1865	100,676	82,085	1893	52,132	49,122
1866	98,890	86,594	1894	42,008	39,597
1867	88,622	79,571	1895	54,349	52,047
1868	64,965	57,662	1896	42,222	39,952
1869	73,325	66,467	1897	35,678	32,822
1870	74,283	67,891	1898	34,395	30,878
1871	71,067	65,591	1899	42,890	38,631
1872	72,763	66,752	1900	45,905	41,848
			1901	39,210	35,535

Quoted in Arnold Schrier, *Ireland and the American Emigration, 1850–1900* (Minneapolis, 1958), Appendix, Table 1, 157.

2. The number of families and persons evicted in Ireland be-
tweeen 1849 and 1882:

	Evicted				Evicted	
Year	Families	Persons	Year	Families	Persons
1849	16,686	90,440	1867	549	2,489
1850	19,949	104,163	1868	637	3,002
1851	13,197	68,023	1869	374	1,741
1852	8,591	43,494	1870	548	2,616
1853	4,833	24,589	1871	482	2,357
1854	2,156	10,794	1872	526	2,476
1855	1,849	9,338	1873	671	3,078
1856	1,108	5,114	1874	726	3,571
1857	1,161	5,475	1875	667	3,323
1858	957	4,643	1876	553	2,550
1859	837	3,872	1877	463	2,177
1860	636	2,985	1878	980	4,679
1861	1,092	5,288	1879	1,238	6,239
1862	1,136	5,617	1880	2,110	10,457
1863	1,734	8,695	1881	3,415	17,341
1864	1,924	9,201	1882	5,201	26,836
1865	942	4,513			
1866	795	3,571	Total	98,723	504,747

Quoted in Michael Davitt, *The Fall of Feudalism in Ireland: Or the Story of the
Land League Revolution* (London, 1904), 100.

APPENDIX B

The statistics on paupers in Ireland (4) during this period illustrate
that the burden of maintaining the poor was considerably lightened,
and the shift from tillage to grazing is readily apparent in the
statistics on what was being cultivated (5) on Irish acreage between
1860 and 1900.

There is an interesting correlation between the figures on paupers
and the figures on emigration quoted earlier. Both sets of figures
are even more revealing when related to the bad harvest years in
Ireland, and especially when related to the bad potato harvest years
of 1850, 1851, 1952, 1961, 1962, 1877, 1878, and 1879. These years
result in an immediate and corresponding increase in paupers and
a corresponding increase, with a time lag, in emigration.

3. Number and percentage of holdings above one acre in Ireland, 1841–1901:

Year	Total Holdings*	1–5 Acres		5–15 Acres		15–30 Acres		Over 30 Acres	
		No. of Holdings	%	No. of Holdings	%	No. of Holdings	%	No. of Holdings	%
1841	691,114†	310,436	44.9	252,799	36.6	79,342	11.5	48,625	7.0
1851	608,066	88,083	15.5	191,854	33.6	141,311	24.8	149,090	26.1
1861	610,045	85,469	15.0	183,931	32.4	141,251	24.8	157,833	27.8
1871	592,590	74,809	13.7	171,383	31.5	138,647	25.5	159,303	29.3
1881	577,739	67,071	12.7	164,045	31.1	135,793	25.8	159,834	30.4
1891	572,640	63,464	12.3	156,661	30.3	133,947	25.9	162,940	31.5
1901	590,175	62,855	12.2	154,418	29.9	134,091	26.0	164,483	31.9

Source: *Agricultural Statistics of Ireland, with detailed report for the year 1901*, p. 15 [Cd. 1170], H.C. 1902, cxvi-Part I.
* Includes holdings of less than one acre.
† Does not include holdings of less than one acre.
Quoted in Schrier, *Ireland and the American Emigration*, Appendix, Table 11, 163.

4. Paupers:

NUMBER OF PAUPERS AND PERCENTAGE OF TOTAL POPULATION IN IRELAND, 1852–95

Year	No. in Workhouses	Percentage of Population	Year	No. in Workhouses	Percentage of Population
1852	166,821	2.60	1874	46,981	0.88
1853	129,401	2.06	1875	45,945	0.87
1854	95,190	1.54	1876	43,652	0.82
1855	79,211	1.30	1877	43,594	0.82
1856	63,235	1.04	1878	47,022	0.88
1857	50,665	0.84	1879	49,996	0.93
1858	45,790	0.76	1880	54,246	1.02
1859	40,380	0.67	1881	52,789	1.03

Year			Year		
1860	41,271	0.69	1882	50,563	0.99
1861	45,136	0.78	1883	50,315	1.00
1862	53,668	0.93	1884	47,625	0.96
1863	57,910	1.01	1885	46,468	0.94
1864	56,525	0.99	1886	46,104	0.94
1865	53,917	0.95	1887	45,488	0.94
1866	50,280	0.90	1888	45,218	0.94
1867	52,154	0.94	1889	43,838	0.93
1868	53,690	0.97	1890	42,517	0.91
1869	52,247	0.94	1891	40,914	0.87
1870	49,186	0.89	1892	40,437	0.87
1871	46,005	0.85	1893	41,160	0.89
1872	45,753	0.85	1894	41,254	0.89
1873	46,711	0.87	1895	40,578	0.89

Quoted in Schrier, *Ireland and the American Emigration*, Appendix, Table 15, 165.

5. Shift from tillage to grazing in Ireland from 1860 to 1900:

Year	Total Area (Statute Acres)	Cultivated Area (Crops & Grasses)	Crops (other than Meadow and Clover)	Meadow & Clover	Grass
1860	20,284,893	15,453,773	4,375,621	1,594,518	9,483,634
1880	20,327,764	15,340,192	3,171,259	1,909,825	10,259,108
1900	20,333,344	15,208,289	2,452,459	2,178,592	10,577,238

Quoted in *Ireland: Industrial and Agricultural*, ed. William P. Coyne (rev. ed., Dublin, 1902), 307.

APPENDIX C

There are no separate national income figures for Ireland. There are, however, decadal estimates of British national income for the whole of the nineteenth century.[53] If Irish national income had grown at the same rate as the British, and if we knew what the proportional relationship between them was at any given time, Irish national income would simply be a constant percentage of the British. Since Irish national income, however, was declining relative to the British in the nineteenth century, the problem becomes one of working out some meaningful declining percentage ratio between 1800 and 1900. We are fortunate in that at both the beginning and the end of the century we have some idea of what the relative proportions in wealth and income were between Britain and Ireland. The Act of Union, which was passed in 1800, had resulted in the amassing of much information as to what would be an equitable financial arrangement between the two contries. Ireland was eventually asked to assume a financial burden in relation to Britain in the ratio of 2:15 or 13.33 per cent.[54] I have, therefore, taken as my starting point that Irish national income in 1800 was some 15 per cent of British national income. In the 1890's a royal commission was appointed to inquire into the financial relations between Britain and Ireland, and especially to determine whether Ireland was being overtaxed in relation to its capacity to pay. Naturally this gave rise to much discussion as to what Ireland's national income actually was. In its "Final Report" in 1895 the commission came to the conclusion that Irish national income stood in relation to British national income in the ratio of 1:20, or 5 per cent.[55]

In the following table, therefore, I have taken the Irish national income in 1800 to be 15 per cent of the British, and in every succeeding decade I reduce that percentage by 1 until I arrive at the figure of 5 per cent in 1900.[56] The results are somewhat crude, but useful, Irish national income figures for the nineteenth century. Further, in this table, I have taken the agricultural component, which remained relatively constant over the course of the century, of British national income and calculated the agricultural component of Irish national income as being 3/10 of the British agricultural component.[57] I arrived at the figure of 3/10 in the following way. In Britain and Ireland in 1900 the areas under cultivation were 32,000,000 and 15,000,000 acres, respectively.[58] On the basis of acreage, therefore, Ireland was in relation to Britain in the ratio

Year	British National Income	Estimated Irish Percentage	Irish National Income	British Agricultural Component of National Income	Irish Aricultural Component of National Income (3/10)
1801	232	15	35	75.5	23
1811	301	14	42	107.5	32
1821	291	13	38	76.0	23
1831	340	12	41	79.5	24
1841	452	11	50	99.9	30
1851	523	10	52	106.5	32
1861	668	9	60	118.8	36
1871	917	8	73	130.4	39
1881	1051	7	74	109.1	33
1891	1288	6	77	110.9	33
1901	1643	5	82	104.6	31

of 15:32, or 47 per cent. Given that Irish agriculture was less efficient, more involved in grazing than tillage, and farther from the immediate market, to translate the acreage ratio into an income ratio is unreal, for it is much too high. The estimate of Deane and Cole, on the other hand, that in the 1900's Ireland accounted for between 20 and 25 per cent of the net output of agricultural seems too low if contemporary estimates are taken into consideration.[59] I have, therefore, taken a figure of ³⁄₁₀ of the British agricultural component to arrive at the Irish agricultural component in my table.

In the accompanying graph, based on my table, I have plotted Irish national income in the nineteenth century and the agricultural component of that national income. The lessons I mean to draw from these curves are noted in the text and footnotes of this article.

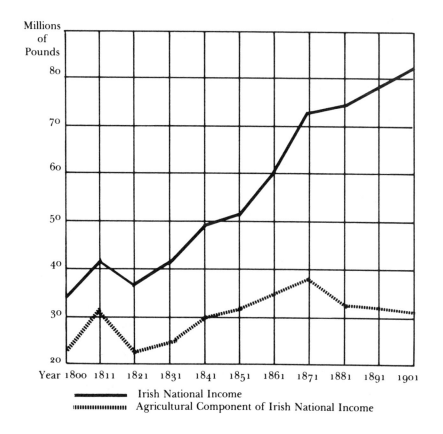

Irish National Income
Agricultural Component of Irish National Income

APPENDIX D

In the following table I have constructed some very crude per capita income figures for Ireland and Britain by dividing estimates of Irish and British national income from Appendix A by estimates of Irish and British populations in the nineteenth century. I have then arbitrarily decided to take the Catholic share of Irish national income as one-half for the whole of the century. This is obviously an overestimation, especially so in the first half of the century, but useful because it provides an upper limit. Even on the basis of these figures the per capita income for Catholics is appalling, especially when it is realized that a marginal subsistence figure must be subtracted from the per capita to learn what was available above subsistence. The Catholic and Protestant shares of Irish national income are the result of taking half of that income and dividing it by the estimated number of Protestants and Catholics in Ireland. The column designated "Margin for Catholics" is the result of taking the subsistence figure at £5 between 1801 and 1851, and graduating at £1 per decade upward until it stands at £10 in 1900. A family of five could subsist on £1 per week or £50 per year in Ireland in about 1900.

APPENDIX E

The problem of determining what was available over and above subsistence of the Catholic share of Irish national income before and after the famine is complicated by the fact that any such determination rests on a number of assumptions that border very nearly on presumptions. We must first assume that the subsistence figure for an individual in Ireland before 1850 was £5 per year and afterward increased £1 per decade until it reached £10 per year in 1901. The second assumption involves making a distinction between those Catholics who lived in a money economy and those who did not, and arriving at some estimate of those who did not relative to those who did. This second assumption, furthermore, is a necessary correlative of the first. If we take the estimated total Catholic population (column 1) and multiply it by £5 (column 4) in any of the decades before the famine, we would arrive at a subsistence figure that would be greater than the estimated Catholic share of national income, which is impossible, and indeed results

Year	Per Capita Income in Ireland	Per Capita Income in Britain	Catholic Share Ireland	Protestant Share Ireland	Margin for Catholics in Ireland
1801	6.7	21.7	4.6	13.0	−.4 (£5)
1811	7.3	24.8	4.6	15.5	−.4 (£5)
1821	5.5	20.5	3.3	13.6	−1.7 (£5)
1831	5.3	20.8	3.5	14.0	−1.5 (£5)
1841	6.1	24.4	3.8	16.1	−1.2 (£5)
1851	7.9	25.1	5.1	19.2	+.1 (£5)
1861	10.4	28.8	6.6	24.0	+.6 (£6)
1871	13.5	35.1	8.9	29.3	+1.9 (£7)
1881	14.4	35.3	9.3	30.8	+1.3 (£8)
1891	16.4	38.9	10.9	34.0	+1.9 (£9)
1901	18.4	44.3	12.4	35.6	+2.4 (£10)

All figures in this table are in pounds.

Year	1 Estimated Catholic Population of Ireland	2 Estimated Catholic Population Less the Subsistence Sector	3 Estimated Catholic Share of National Income (½) in Millions of £	4 Estimated Amount for Individual's Subsistence in a Money Economy in Ireland	5 Total Subsistence Figure for Ireland in Millions of £ (col. 2 by col. 4)	6 Amount Available over and above Subsistence for Investment (col. 3 minus col. 5)
1801	3,900,000	2,600,000(1/5)	18	5	13.0	5.0
1811	4,600,000	3,100,000(1/3)	21	5	15.5	5.5
1821	5,800,000	3,900,000(1/3)	19	5	19.5	−0.5
1831	6,300,000	4,200,000(1/3)	21	5	20.0	1.1
1841	6,650,000	4,450,000(1/3)	25	5	22.2	2.8
1851	5,150,000	4,120,000(1/5)	26	5	20.6	5.4
1861	4,500,000	4,000,000(1/10)	30	6	24.0	6.0
1871	4,150,000	3,900,000(1/15)	37	7	27.3	9.7
1881	3,950,000	3,750,000(1/20)	37	8	30.0	7.0
1891	3,550,000	3,550,000(0/0)	39	9	32.0	7.0
1901	3,300,000	3,300,000(0/0)	41	10	33.0	8.0

in the negative figures in the table in Appendix D. The negative factor seems to be that a large proportion of the Catholic population not only merely subsisted, or even existed outside the money economy, but was actually nonproductive and even parasitic on their potato patches. The real question, of course, is how large was this group. For the years before the famine I have estimated it as ⅓ the Catholic population, and after the famine, when it was gradually broken up by emigration, I have reduced it decade by decade by ⅕, ⅒, 1/15, 1/20, % (column 2). There is no doubt that the factor of ⅓ for the fifty years before the famine is truer as we approach the famine than earlier in the century, and a graduated series, ⅐, ⅙, ⅕, ¼, ⅓, from 1800 to 1840 might be more appropriate. There is also no doubt that the £5 per year subsistence figure might also be modified or even graduated for these years, but until we have more information as to what subsistence figures actually were in the nineteenth century, and until we have some estimates of how large the subsistence and nonproductive sectors of the Catholic population were, it is best to proceed on the basis of constant, even if somewhat unreal, figures so as to be able to open the discussion with a point of departure. According to column 6 in this table, therefore, the amount available for investment over and above subsistence between 1800 and 1850 was £143,000,000 or £2,860,000 per year. For the fifty years after 1850, the amount available was £356,000,000 or £7,120,000 per year.

NOTES

[1] Patrick Curtis to Michael Blake, July 23, 1825, *Scritture riferite nei congressi, Irlanda, 24, fols. 470–71, Archives of the Society for the Propagation of the Faith, Rome.*

[2] *Freeman's Journal* (Dublin), June 3, 1901, quoted in Michael J. F. McCarthy, *Priests and People in Ireland* (Dublin, 1903), 35.

[3] The best available discussion of this problem of maritime and subsistence economies is in Patrick Lynch and John Vaizey, *Guiness's Brewery in the Irish Economy, 1759–1876* (Cambridge, Eng., 1960), 9–17.

[4] An Irish priest asked Alexis de Tocqueville in Galway in July 1835: "Sir, do you know what it is that prevents the poor from starving to death in Ireland?" "It is the poor," the priest answered, and added, "A farmer who has only thirty acres and who harvests only a hundred bushels of potatoes, puts aside a fifth of his harvest annually to be distributed among those unfortunates who are the most terribly in need. . . . In order to give alms the farmer will stint his land of manure and wear rags, and his wife will sleep on straw and his children not go to school." (Alexis de Tocqueville, *Journeys to England and Ireland*, ed. J. P. Mayer [London, 1958], 164–65.)

[5] With regard to the increase and the distribution of population in Ireland before 1847, respectively, the best discussions are K. H. Connell, *The Population of Ireland, 1780–1845* (Oxford, Eng., 1950), and T. W. Freeman, *Pre-Famine Ireland: A Study in Historical Geography* (Manchester, Eng., 1957). Freeman presents a detailed series of population density maps constructed from government ordnance survey maps (six inches to one mile) published between 1833 and 1844.

[6] See Appendix A.

[7] See Appendix B.

[8] Nulty to Kirby, May 29, 1879, Tobias Kirby Papers, Archives of the Irish College, Rome.

[9] The best general discussion of the last quarter of the nineteenth century is Barbara Solow, *The Land Question and the Irish Economy, 1870–1903* (Cambridge, Mass., 1971).

[10] *Acta*, 169 fols. 135–44, Archives of the Society for the Propagation of the Faith, Rome.

[11] *Ibid.*

[12] *Scritture riferite nei congressi, Irlanda*, 18, fols. 262–63.

[13] See Appendix C and accompanying graph and table.

[14] *Scritture riferite nei congressi, Irlanda*, 30, fols. 132–35: "Brevi Rilievi sopra il sistema d'insegnamento misto che si cerca di stabilire in Irlanda nei collegi cosi detti della Regina."

[15] *Ibid.*

[16] Myles O'Reilly, *Progress of Catholicity in Ireland in the Nineteenth Century* (Dublin, 1865). These various estimates on what property the Church acquired before 1850 are further supported by an independent estimate of what was acquired in the all-important archdiocese of Dublin between 1822 and 1852. "An estimate made out with great care represents the amount of property moveable and immoveable acquired by religion in the Catholic Archbishopric of Dublin, during his [Daniel Murray] incumbency, as exceeding considerably 'bp1,200,000." (William Meagher, *Life of Archbishop Murray* [Doublin, 1853], 116.)

[17] Maher to Cullen, Feb. 21, 1843, Paul Cullen Papers, Archives of the Irish College, Rome.

[18] John Healy, *Maynooth College: Its Centenary History* (Dublin, 1895), Appendix XVIII, 740–41:

[19] Tocqueville, *Journeys to England and Ireland*, ed. Mayer, 142–43.

[20] *Ibid.*, 158–59.

[21] Maher to Cullen, Apr. 18, 1842, Cullen Papers.

[22] Maher to Cullen, Jan. 2, 1842, *ibid.*

[23] G. Locker Lampson, A Consideration of the State of Ireland in the Nineteenth Century (New York, 1907), 265: "Between October 1849 and August 1857 the number of purchasers or new landlords amounted to 7,489, of which 7,180 were natives of Ireland, and 309 Englishmen, Scotchmen or foreigners. The total sum realized by these sales amounted to £20,475,956 of which £17,639,731 was Irish capital." See also O'Reilly, *Progress of Catholicity*, 19–20: "It was only a very few years before the close of the eighteenth century that Catholics acquired the power of purchasing land; and consequently the only Catholic landed proprietors in Ireland were those few whose property had escaped confiscation during the three hundred years of the penal laws. The famine of 1845 ruined an immense number of proprietors; and of their estates which were sold a large portion was purchased by Catholics who had become rich. In 1861 the number of landed proprietors in Ireland was 8,412, of whom forty-two per cent were Catholics." Two questions naturally arise out of the Lampson quote: how many of the Irish purchasers were Catholics, and how much land did they buy? For example, they could have made up 90 per cent of the purchasers and bought only 10 per cent of the land on the market. Though 42 per cent of the Irish landlords, therefore, were Catholic in 1861, as

O'Reilly points out, the real question is how much land did they own. The question becomes even more complicated when one asks where they owned it, for ten thousand acres in Meath would be quite different from ten thousand acres in Connemara. A shrewd contemporary observer, Cullen, however, who has been promoted to the archbishopric of Armagh in 1849, writing Alessandro Barnabó, secretary of the *Congregatio de propaganda fide* in Rome, on October 10, 1851, from Drogheda, explained that though the mass of the people were still miserable in their poverty, £3,000,000 in land had already changed hands, and that in the long run it would tell to the advantage of the Catholics who were buying in. (*Scritture riferite nei congressi, Irlanda*, XXX, fols. 725–26.) Until, however, we know much more about Irish land purchase in the nineteenth century than we know now, it would be a hardy man who would assert too much.

[24] See section on "De Bonis Ecclesiasticis," esp. Arts. 5–9, *Decreta, Synodi Nationalis totius Hiberniae Thurlesiae Habitae Anno MDCCCL* (Dublin, 1851), 50–51.

[25] *Ibid.*, 40: "De Parochia"—"16. Cum nemo militans Deo negotiis saecularibus se implicat, cumque periculum sit ne ii qui latifundia conducant, tempus in iis colendis quod spirituali populi curae debitum est, impendant, vetamus ne quis parochus conducat aut retineat plusquam quindecim jugera terrae sine consensu Episcopi./17. Vicarii autum parochorum non conducant ullam portionem agrorum, nisi accedat Episcopi consensus."

[26] *Decreta, Synodi Plenariae Episcoporum Hiberniae, Habitae apud Maynutiam, An. 1875* (Dublin, 1877), 111, 126–27.

[27] Kiernan to Kirby, Feb. 28, 1868, Kirby Papers.

[28] Keane to Kirby, Feb. 20, 1869, *ibid.*

[29] McCarthy to Kirby, Feb. 6, 1877, *ibid.*

[30] Browne to O'Riordan, Nov. 29, 1910, Michael O'Riordan Papers, Archives of the Irish College, Rome.

[31] See McCarthy, *Priests and People*, 625, for appendix comparing clerical population to Catholic population using the censuses of 1861 and 1901. In 1861 there were 5,955 priests, monks, and nuns for a Catholic population of 4,505,265; in 1901 there were 14,145 clergy for a population of 3,308,661.

[32] P. J. Brophy, "Irish Missionaries," *The Carlovian, The Carlow College Magazine an Annual Review* (1951), 7, Table B, "Showing the Destination of Theological Students of Carlow College":

Year	Number of Ecclesiastical Students for Service In Ireland	Number of Ecclesiastical Students for Service Outside Ireland
1836–37	43	—
1837–38	39	1
1838–39	49	—
1839–40	45	—
1940–41	58	—
1841–42	70	—
1842–43	66	—
1844–45	—	10
1845–46	47	14
1846–47	47	22
1847–48	55	26
1848–49	51	31
1849–50	38	28

Year	Number of Ecclesiastical Students for Service In Ireland	Number of Ecclesiastical Students for Service Outside Ireland
1850–51	24	27
1851–52	29	24
1852–53	20	19
1853–54	10	25
1880–81	32	46
1881–82	35	45
1889–90	37	63
1892–93	37	73
1897–98	15	112
1907–08	12	112

See also O'Reilly, *Progress of Catholicity*, 16–17: All Hallows, which was founded in Dublin in 1842, had by 1864 "220 students, who are being educated for the foreign missions; and since its first institution this establishmemt has sent out 400 priests." This is to say nothing of the religious orders in Ireland that had houses "where their members are educated for the priesthood: such are the calced Carmelites, Dominicans, Augustinians, Cistercians, Jesuits, Vincentians, Passionists, Redemptorists, and Oblates of Mary." Most of these young men were also destined for the foreign missions.

[33] The evidence to support these figures is much too cumbersome to present in a footnote. Each bishop in Ireland usually forwarded his Peter's pence through the rector of the Irish College in Rome. I have tabulated all the contributions mentioned in the correspondence between 1860 and 1919 from each of the dioceses in Ireland. None of the resulting series of figures for each diocese are complete, and some of the series are very spotty, but with some judicious projection a general average of £10,000 can be easily deduced. In 1860 the Papal States were invaded by the army of the King of Sardinia, and Ireland responded with the launching of the Peter's pence collection and the recruiting of a papal brigade. Cullen, who had been transferred from Armagh to Dublin in 1852, reported to Kirby in Rome that the collection in Ireland would reach £80,000. (Cullen to Kirby, July 28, 1860, Kirby Papers.)

[34] Meagher, *Life of Archbishop Murray*. By 1853 Ireland had contributed something just less than £70,000, over a third of which was contributed by the diocese of Dublin alone. O'Reilly, *Progress of Catholicity*, 26, reported that by 1864 Ireland had contributed £149,124 to the Society for the Propagation of the Faith.

[35] The culmination of all this was reached when Rome issued new regulations in 1909 for Ireland with regard to borrowing money. Any debt over £20 and under £400 could be contracted only with the consent of the local bishop. Any debt contracted over £400, however, had to be cleared with Rome. The bishop of Waterford, R. A. Sheehan, in writing O'Riordan, rector of the Irish College, complained that most Catholic institutions in Ireland had no working capital since their ordinary capital was usually tied up. Resort to the credit facilities of banks, therefore, was necessary to carry on until these institutions were either paid by the state for duties fulfilled, or their investments paid their dividends. (Sheehan to O'Riordan, Dec. 28, 1909, O'Riordan Papers.)

[36] McCarthy, *Priests and People*, 108–49. Most of the bequests and legacies cited by McCarthy were published in the Irish newspapers between August 1901 and April 1902.

[37] Leahy to Kirby, Nov. 15, 1864, Kirby Papers.
[38] Bradley to Kelly, June 3, 1897, Michael Kelly Papers, Archives of the Irish College, Rome.
[39] Henry to O'Riordan, Nov. 21, 1906, O'Riordan Papers.
[40] Henry to O'Riordan, Dec. 10, 1906, *ibid.*
[41] Henry to O'Riordan, Dec. 21, 1907, *ibid.*
[42] Henry to O'Riordan, Jan. 2, 1908, *ibid.*
[43] Logue to Kelly, May 1, 1896, Kelly Papers.
[44] See Appendix C.
[45] O'Reilly, *Progress of Catholocity*, 18–19.
[46] *Ibid.*, 20.
[47] See graph, Appendix C.
[48] Catholic Defense Association, *Light on the Local Government Board* (Dublin, 1901):

Permanent Staff, Local Government Board

I. Nominated Positions:		Catholics
Commissioner	1	£1,200
General Inspectors	3	1,700
Medical Inspectors	3	1,700
Bacteriologist	1	250
Engineering Inspectors	nil	—
Auditors	5	2,700
	13	7,550

Average salary of the above (13)   £580-15s.-od.

II. Nominated Positions:		Protestants
Commissioners	2	£3,000
Secretary	1	900
General Inspectors	6	4,200
Medical Inspectors	4	2,800
Engineering Inspectors	4	2,150
Auditors	12	6,800
Audit Clerk	1	425
Secretary, Vaccine Department	1	300
Pharmacist	1	300
Legal Advisor	1	800
Legal Assistant	1	500
	34	22,225

Average salary of the above (34)   £653-13s.-od.

III. Competitive Positions:		Catholics
Principal Clerks	2	£1,300
Deputy Principal	1	480
Upper Division	3	1,140
Clerk in Charge of Accounts	1	425
Registrar	1	400
Superintendent, Statistical Branch	1	350
Local Stocks Clerk	1	329
Superintendent, Index Branch	1	316
Private Secretary to Vice-President	1	210
Higher, Grade Second Division	3	900
Second Division	28	3,080
	43	8,930

Average salary of the above (43)		£207-13s.-od.
Average salary of the first 15		£390-0s.-od.

IV. Competitive Positions:		Protestants
Assistant Secretary	1	£ 700
Principal Clerks	2	1,300
Deputy Principals	2	1,440
Upper Division	7	2,660
Higher Grade, Second Division	1	300
Second Division, Ordinary	11	1,610
	25	7,610

Average salary of above (25)		£304-8s.-od.
Average salary of the first 14		£457-3s.-od.

[49] *The Leader* (Dublin), Jan. 30, 1904. This weekly organ of Catholic middle-class public opinion in Ireland complained, for example, about the discrimination against Irishmen and Catholics in the Provincial Bank of Ireland. "The Provincial Bank of Ireland was founded in 1824. Its original staff consisted largely of Scotchmen, and the principle officers of the establishment are of the same nationality. The present Directorate of the Bank consists of 10 Directors, of whom one is an Irish Catholic, and the remaining are English or Scotch Protestants. We shall now analyze the staff of the Bank giving the salary—approximate or actual—in the cases of the general staff, and the approximate totals of the other staffs."

Grouped Results

	Creed	Number	Salary Totals
I. General Staff	Protestants	5	£ 4,500
	Catholics	nil	nil
II. Managerial Staff	Protestants	52	£22,050
	Catholics	2	510
III. Tellers and Accountants	Protestants	75	£14,350
	Catholics	8	1,530
IV. Clerical Staff	Protestants	170	£17,285
	Catholics	19	1,625
V. Summary	Protestants	302	£58,185
	Catholics	29	3,665
VI. Average Annual Salaries	Protestants		£192-13s.-od.
	Catholics		£126-7s.-od.

[50] See Appendix D.

[51] See Appendix E.

[52] E.g., *Freeman's Journal Church Commission* (Dublin, 1868), 386–87: "Before I proceed to give in one summary all the items of Catholic expenditure supplied by voluntary effort, let me glance hastily at those I have been compelled to omit. The omissions include all the sums contributed to convents, convent schools, and orphanages; the support of the churches and chapels of the religious orders, of religious confraternities, guilds, & c., and all the orphanages, asylums, refuges, with the exception of the few statistics relative to those in the city of Dublin. In addition, I may mention sums collected annually in Ireland for Catholic purposes in England,

which are very considerable. I have known £1,000 collected at one time in one Irish diocese for a single convent in England:—"

SUMMARY OF CATHOLIC EXPENDITURE IN IRELAND

Expenditure on Erection of Buildings Since 1800.

In 26 Dioceses,	1,842 Churches	£3,198,627
"	218 Converts, includes Schools, &c., attached	1,061,215
"	41 Colleges and Seminaries	309,018
"	44 Hospitals, Asylums, &c.	147,135
	Add for two dioceses not returned	306,000
"	600 Parochial Houses	300,000
"	2,990 Non-vested Catholic Schoolhouses	299,000
"	70 Establishments of Christian Brothers	70,000
Total		£5,690,995

Annual Expediture.

1. Bishops and Parochial Clergy	£340,480
2. Regular Clergy	55,000
3. Maintenance, Repairs, and Extension of Churches	116,050
4. Catholic Hospitals, Orphanages, Asylums, &c.	
5. Colleges, Seminaries, and Schools supported by contributions, estimated at	250,500
Total	£762,030

[53] Phyllis Deane and W. A. Cole, *British Economic Growth, 1688–1959: Trends and Structure* (Cambridge, Eng., 1962), 166.

[54] Sir James O'Connor, *History of Ireland 1798–1924* (2 vols., London, 1925), I, 122–23.

[55] "Final Report, Royal Commission on the financial relations between Great Britain and Ireland," Parliamentary Papers, cmd. 8262, 1896. The best discussion of this whole question is found in Thomas Lough, *England's Wealth Ireland's Poverty* (London, 1897), 104–11; see also the Earl of Dunraven, *The Crisis in Ireland: An Account of the Present Condition of Ireland and Suggestions towards Reform* (London, 1905).

[56] Deane and Cole, *British Economic Growth,* 168: "The Irish residuals seem to be about the right order of magnitude in terms of the United Kingdom estimates: that is to say they fall between 15 and 20 per cent of the United Kingdom total before the famine and its aftermath, and between 5 and 9 per cent after."

[57] *Ibid.,* 166. See this table for agricultural component of British national income.

[58] *Ireland: Industrial and Agricultural,* ed. William P. Coyne (Dublin, 1902), 307.

[59] Deane and Cole, *British Economic Growth,* 174.

II

The Devotional Revolution
in Ireland, 1850-75

"If you knew," a Waterford priest wrote Tobias Kirby, the new rector of the Irish College in Rome, on January 3, 1850, "all there is to remedy, all the evil there is to check!"[1] "We have not had," he further explained to Kirby, referring to the decline in clerical discipline after the famine, "a Conference here since the beginning of the distress, four years now probably—& but *one* retreat all that time & everyone doing & thinking & speaking as it listeth him, & no one to prevent it." The occasion for this lament was the recent and encouraging news from Rome that Paul Cullen, Kirby's predecessor as rector of the Irish College, had just been appointed archbishop of Armagh and the accompanying rumor that the new primate had also been armed with the power of apostolic delegate by Pius IX and instructed to summon a national synod for the better government and regulation of the Irish Church. More than a quarter of a century after Cullen's arrival in Ireland, his cousin and protégé, Patrick Francis Moran, the bishop of Ossory, was able to report to Kirby in a matter-of-fact way from Kilkenny during the course of a letter that "we ended two small Missions in two of our city Churches on Sunday last, preparatory for Christmas."[2] "Nothing," he further explained, "could be more consoling than the great piety of our poor people. All without exception approached the Holy Sacraments." "At my Mass on Sunday in the Cathedral," Moran emphasized in conclusion, "there were about *1000 men* at Holy Communion." In the nearly thirty years that he faithfully served Rome in Ireland, Paul Cardinal Cullen not only reformed the Irish Church but, what was perhaps even more important, in the process of reforming that Church he spearheaded the consolidation of a devotional revolution. The great mass of the Irish people became practicing Catholics, which they have uniquely and essentially remained both at home and abroad down to the present day.

The measure of Cullen's achievement naturally depends on how much had been done to make practicing Catholics of the Irish people before his arrival in Ireland in early 1850. What resources, in terms of plant and personnel, had been available to the Church for the encouragement and sustaining of devotional practices? And what was the character of as well as the example given by the Irish clergy to their flocks in promoting such practices? Corporately characterizing some 2,500 priests or even only some thirty bishops over a period of fifty years is obviously as hazardous as it is difficult.[3] And given the still raw state of the available evidence any systematic analysis of the resources of the Irish Church before the famine is as yet virtually impossible.[4] While the evidence is admittedly not in a condition, either quantitatively or qualitatively, to yield a consensus satisfactory to historians, it may be useful to attempt to structure a frame in which that developing body of evidence may be more intelligently researched and analyzed.

Since the quantitative problem of the number of clergy is relatively the easiest to come to terms with, perhaps it would be best to deal with it first. In 1800 there were about 1,850 priests, including some 26 bishops, in Ireland for a Catholic population estimated at 3,900,000, or roughly a ratio of one priest to 2,100 faithful. There were also in 1800 only 122 nuns in Ireland, which if reduced to a ratio divides out at the meaningless proportion of one nun to 32,000.[5] By 1850 the ratio between priests and people was still about one to 2,100, with over 2,500 priests available for something more than 5,000,000 Catholics. The nun population, however, had by 1850 increased thirteenfold, from 122 to over 1,500 in fifty years, and instead of one nun for 32,000 people, there was one nun for every 3,400 Catholics.[6] These figures, of course, in themselves are actually misleading because they mask the effects of the outstanding social tragedy in modern Irish history—the Great Famine. Between 1800 and 1840 the Catholic population had risen to 6,500,000, an increase of about 2,600,000, and probably increased another 250,000 by 1846.[7] By 1850, as a result of the famine and its aftermath, this population of nearly seven million in 1846 was reduced by some two million in four years.[8]

When it is realized that in 1840 there were only about 2,150 priests for a Catholic population of 6,500,000, or merely one priest for every 3,000 people, and that there were, furthermore, only about 1,000 nuns, or one for every 6,500 faithful, it becomes rather obvious that in the decade of the forties, and especially in the years before 1846, the Church in the face of incredibly adverse economic circumstances responded impressively, even if tardily, to the challenge of growing numbers by increasing the clerical population by some 400 priests and over 500 nuns—a twenty and fifty per cent increase respectively in ten years.[9] After 1840 and before the famine, therefore, the priests were gaining slowly and the nuns rapidly in relation to a population that was still increasing, though at a progressively declining rate. Patently, this relative increase in the clerical population meant little in practical terms before the famine, but when the population was suddenly reduced by nearly two million between 1846 and 1850 the whole clerical-lay numerical relationship was dramatically transformed, and what may have been only a short-term tendency rooted in a heroic institutional effort to increase the clerical population between 1840 and 1846, became in the next one hundred years a basic secular trend in Ireland. What emerges, then, even from this cursory analysis, is simply that before the famine any effective service on the part of the clergy was severely limited by the sheer weight of lay numbers, and that up to 1840, at least, the situation had been getting progressively worse.

But if the shortage of priests was so serious, perhaps the numerical deficiency was compensated for in some measure by the quality of their performance. Without more detailed biographical information about the nearly five thousand priests who served the Irish Church between 1800 and 1845, however, any estimate of their corporate character and conduct must remain largely impressionistic. There is, in fact, a strong bias in the available evidence in favor of extreme presentations. If, for example, one confined oneself only to reading the correspondence between Ireland and Rome in the archives of the Society for the Propagation of the Faith (Propaganda Fide), where nearly all the dirty Irish clerical linen was washed, the clergy might easily be characterized as drunken, disorderly, and immoral, or worse. While it is obviously impossible to present in any meaningful way more than fifty years of evidence from the Propaganda archives, perhaps a few examples will not only suffice to show what the nature of the evidence is, but also what the problems are in evaluating it. "I expect to leave this town tomorrow," Edward Dillon, the archbishop of Tuam, explained from Tuam in County Galway, on January 7, 1805, to John Collins, one of his priests, "and do not intend to return till Lent." "Previous to my departure," he warned Collins, "I cannot help reminding you of the advice I gave you when you were last at this house."

I am positively determined not to tolerate any whiskey drinking or other publick irregularities amongst my clergy. . . . Let me observe to you finally that if you wish to continue in Dunmore or to be employed in the ministry in this Diocese you must learn to sett a higher value on the sacred character with which you are invested than you have hitherto done. Particularly you must not be known to associate with such persons as Math^w. Martin's or Martin's Strumpet's; much less should you church such persons. I often advised Frank Burke and his Coajutor he vainly tought that I would confine myself to unavailing advice, beware of meeting the fate of the former the later is tolerated merely thro necessity for a few months.[10]

"A Rev^d. M^r. Corbett, a priest of my Diocese," James O'Shaughnessy, bishop of Killaloe, reported to his agent in Rome from Ennis in County Clare, on November 27, 1815, "has been charged with adultery, and with having occasioned the separation of man and wife." "The case seemed so clear against him," O'Shaughnessy explained, "that he ought to have submitted and retired, but in place of doing so, he loudly called for a public trial."

During this trial more perjury and wickedness was practiced than in any Civil Court in the world. Some turbulent and disorderly priests made common cause with M^r. Corbett, and I am informed they joined in a remonstrance to the Holy See, alledging that the sentence passed by the pious and learned D^r. Wright was not founded in justice. My own humble opinion is that there was already too much of this shocking business, and that our Holy Religion wou^d be less-wounded, and less scandal given, by not stiring the embers further.

The unfortunate woman seems within one month of her accouchment tho her husband left the country 15 months ago. If with your usual attention you would make known the circumstances to the Sacred Congregation, and put a stop to any further proceedings, it would be rendering an essential service to the Catholic Religion of this poor persecuted country.

"When anything final," O'Shaughnessy suggested, "comes to your knowledge I request to hear from you." "I am sure," he concluded encouragingly, "you will give it every necessary attention, of which I will be *mindful*."[11]

The third and final example of the nature of the evidence in the Propaganda archives concerning the conduct of the clergy is a long letter from James Murphy, bishop of Clogher, to Lorenzo Litta, cardinal prefect of Propaganda, dated Monaghan, April 2, 1818, thanking His Eminence for the news of the appointment of a coadjutor with the right to succeed him in Clogher, but also taking exception to the cardinal's suggestion that he should be less severe regarding several of his priests with whom he was in serious litigation at Rome. "And now permit, My Lord," Murphy began his peroration politely, "with the most profound deference, however, for your Eminence and the Sacred Congregation, to say a few words on the treatment I conceive myself to have received from the Sacred Congregation,

Your Eminence may recollect, that in the year 1814, when heavy charges were preferred against me to His Holiness, and two appeals lodged against me, one of them by Priest Maginn, since deceased, on account of having suspended him for *Turpia in Tribunali*; the other by Priest Goodwin having published to the world, and prefered and inscribed to me a *Libellum Accusatorium*, in which he charged a highly respectable and zealous priest with having revealed the confession of his penitant, and in which he also charged two other pastors, the most respectable in the Diocese, with having cooperated in said wicked act. At that time your Eminence sent two commissions to my then metropolitan, the most Rev[d] Richard O'Reilly, the one to examine narrowly into the said charges and report the result to his Holiness; the other to try the appeals and pass a definitive sentence on them—Both these commissions my metropolitan executed, and after a strict scrutiny into the charges against me, he told me, he reported them unfounded and calumnious—relative to the two appeals, he pronounced definitively, as empowered, that my suspensions were just and necessary in both cases—Now what I feel for and consider *severe*, is, that I, or, indeed, any other bishop should be exposed, draged publickly and shamefully from tribunal to tribunal and tried a second time on matters that were already definitively disposed of: for though my metropolitan erred in not depriving Priest Maginn of his parish, yet, his sentence, which bound that unfortunate man on oath never to hear the confession of a female, not only justified but even proved the necessity of my suspension—to these matters I beg leave to add, that your Eminence sent a commission to my metropolitan in the year 1816, in consequence of an appeal lodged by a Priest Duffy, a curate, and, of course, without any ordinary jurisdiction, against me, for my having interdicted him from exercising certain pastoral functions in despite of his parish priest, and for having suspended him afterwards for his contumacy, in not attending citations I sent him to appear before me, and account for his exercising all and every pastoral function in defiance of my interdict, and for his, besides, raising the people in open rebellion against their lawful pastor—Your Eminence, I say, sent such commission to my metropolitan with orders to cite the parties, and after hearing us, to report the result, together with his own opinion, to your Eminence—I, of course, obeyed the citation though labouring under infirmities and having upwards of sixty Italian miles to make, and having besides to bring necessary witnesses with me at heavy expenses, some thirty, some eighty and some an hundred miles. My metropolitan, after examining me and my witnesses in the presence of the appellant, called on him to rebut what I had proved, when he was answered by the appellant in a highly disrespectful and taunting tone, that he would not, nor would he, he said, answer a single question that he put him— my metropolitan made, of course, his report on this obvious and self evident case, and the Sacred Congregation, notwithstanding, gave it in charge a second time to the Visitor Apostolic—This I confess, I consider also *severe*.[12]

"It has exposed me," Murphy maintained, "to additional heavy expenses, for the appellant, Priest Duffy, nor indeed any one of the other appellants, though they brought on the suits never paid a single sou of the expenses attendant on the different commissions." "It has, besides," he declared further, "by puting off and prolonging the decision, given them the assurance to expose and villify me and my administration frequently, in one of the most publickly circulating journals in this kingdom, and of threatening me openly and repeatedly with civil suits; so that I may justly say with the Apostle, *Spectaculum Facti Sumus* &c—" "All this publick abuse," Murphy concluded dryly, "I bore without an answer in the hope that God will give me an account for it [in] a better world."

If, on the other hand, one turns from the Propaganda archives to a perusal of the various pious lives of the Irish clergy for the same period, the result is simply a hagiographical headache, or worse.[13] The truth, alas, is not even found by invoking that favorite and prudent device in such circumstances—the *via media*. What happened between 1800 and 1845 is that the character and conduct of the clergy, which certainly left a great deal to be desired at the beginning of the period, was gradually and uniformly improved. By 1830 the worst was over, since the Irish bishops with the help of Rome finally secured the upper hand over their priests.[14] From 1830 the improvement, though still uneven, depending as it did on the character and strength of will of each individual bishop, was at all events steady. The improvement, however, does not appear to have been simply a function of the bishops' authority in time; it seems to have been a reflection of geographical circumstances as well. The improvement was most rapid and sustained in the ecclesiastical province of Dublin, while the deportment of the clergy in Cashel, Armagh, and Tuam was less and less satisfactory from one to the next.

On the occasion of the funeral of the archbishop of Dublin, Daniel Murray, at the end of February 1852, William Meagher delivered an oration in which he reflected on the practical improvement of the Catholic population of Dublin. He graphically described the conditions prevailing in Dublin some forty-two years earlier when Murray had been raised to the episcopal dignity.

The morals of the people of Dublin, Catholics among the rest, were hideously corrupted. The riches daily scattered through her streets in handfuls, to purchase the luxuries of an opulent, and profuse, and dissolute aristocracy; the easy and plentiful earnings of flourishing manufacture, and of extensive and successful commerce, were seized every hour, through a series of years, for indulgence of vilest libertinism, and wildest extravagance. Vices, too gross to be more than alluded to, stalked through the streets shamelessly—the drunkard raved without obstruction, and the blasphemer shouted his impiety, and the gambler squandered in nights of dissipation what his days of toil had accumulated. And, strange to say, and suggestive of many a sad and solemn reflection, there was in our city as large an amount of physical wretchedness, particularly among the lower ranks, then as now—as much squalid poverty—as much shivering nakedness—as much famine-stricken emaciation—as many ruined families—as many houseless orphans! Vice did more to fill the town with the agonies of human suffering than famine, and plague, and abject poverty have wrought in these latter days of woe. Flatter not yourselves, My Brethren, that these excesses and their direful effects were confined to sectarians; they were as rife, if not more so, amongst ourselves. Nor, unless by some standing social and religious miracle, could it be otherwise. Amid opportunities so numerous—examples so seductive—temptations so violent—with but a handful of clergy and a dozen small, mean, and incommodious chapels to second the proverbial faith and innate pious tendencies of the people, what wonder that the multitude was hurried away in this torrent of iniquity? And the mortifying truth is, that in Dublin, at the period alluded to, amid many Catholics there were but few practical Christians; very few whose lives supplied that substantial and only unerring proof of profitable attachment to the faith—the constant and regular frequentation of the holy sacraments. As the climax of her griefs religion had to weep for the first time, perhaps, in this land, over the faltering fidelity and submission of many a son, led astray by the phrenzy of recent revolution, and the false liberality of the day, and the desolating philosophism of France.[15]

There appears to be, moreover, a correlation between the conduct of the clergy in these ecclesiastical provinces of Dublin, Cashel, Armagh, and Tuam and their relative wealth as well as the extent to which each was urban and rural in terms of Catholic population. Furthermore, though the evidence is still very sketchy, the clergy appointed to the town parishes appear to have been better educated than those assigned to the country parishes.[16]

But the application of episcopal authority, the relative wealth of the Catholic communities, the extent of urbanization, and the educational level of the clergy were not the only determinants of social behavior. The moral and social values of the community and the pressure the community applied in terms of what it considered to be right or wrong also affected clerical conduct. The principal vices among the clergy were drunkenness, women, and avarice. Interestingly enough, while this seems to be the order of their importance among the bishops in their efforts to impose discipline, it does not appear to be the order of their importance either before or after the famine as far as the laity who cared were concerned. Among a land-hungry and poverty-stricken peasantry avarice was the deadliest of the deadly sins, while lust and drunkenness were viewed with a more understanding, even if disapproving, eye.[17] The seriousness of the problem of clerical avarice vis-à-vis the faithful, for example, was certainly reflected in early nineteenth-century Ireland in the need of the bishops of the province of Dublin to set up by statute a uniform tariff for clerical dues at their diocesan synods in the summer of 1831. The tariff, however, not only gives a comprehensive glimpse of what was thought to be a fair and proper remuneration for the various services rendered by the clergy but also details an interesting summary of the clergy's sources of income.

1. Baptism—shopkeepers and farmers	o	5	o
Do. poor labourers	o	2	6
2. Marriages—shopkeepers and farmers	2	o	o
3. Licenses for do	o	10	o
Marriages for poor labourers	1	o	o
Licenses for do	o	5	o
4. Masses for dead sung, to shopkeepers and farmers—			
Parish priest	o	15	o
Every other priest	o	10	o
Any other priest who does not officiate	o	5	o

5. Masses, not sung	o	10	o
Masses for dead, to poor labourers	o	5	o
6. Private masses	o	2	o
7. Collections after marriages—these must be voluntary according to the stations of the parties, they may vary from £1 to £100, or more.			
8. Dues at stations—these Dr. Murray informs us are the chief support of the priests; they cannot be called voluntary, for custom makes them compulsory; they are contributed by every person who can give anything, and vary from one shilling to five, as the Editor is informed, say the lowest average from the population of Ireland who attend stations and confessions	o	1	6

9. Fortuitous emoluments—of these, at least one great source of revenue, is masses for delivering the souls from purgatory of those who are dead and buried, left either by will or given by relations of deceased, or, what is very common, given by the poor creatures themselves, for masses before they die, and to benefit their souls when they are gone,—of these it is impossible to calculate the amount.

10. The collecting of corn from the people. This is sometimes commuted for money, and is valued at 1s. 6d. per house, or more.[18]

More particularly, the parishioners from Kilcommen Erris, near Belmullet in County Mayo, in the diocese of Killala, petitioned the pope in early 1840 about the abuses to which they were subject from the local clergy. Their petition comprised some fifteen heads of complaint, and like so many other documents in the Propaganda archives it was the product of a fierce local struggle for power, with the contending parties prepared to say and to write the worst about their opponents. The crucial aspect of this document, therefore, is not indeed whether the charges made in it were necessarily true, but rather that the charges made in it are a serious comment on what the mores and values of the person or persons who wrote it actually were.

To Our Most Holy Father in God Pope Gregory the XVI Successor of Saint Peter and Vicar of Jesus Christ upon Earth. . . .

6thly that the poor uneducated peasantry of the parish generally feel not only scandalised but actually horrified at the not merely tyrannical, but unchristian like conduct of the Rev^d Mr. Conway towards them during the Confessions. When a poor, but pious, humble, contrite penitent presents himself before the altar of reconciliation bewailing his offences, and with devout compunction soliciting to be admitted to the Paschal or Christmas distribution of the Bread of Life—if he has not money to propitiate the avaricious ire of the Revd Mr Conway, he is not quietly dismissed as being too poor and contemptible for enjoying the Celestial benefits; but he is scolded, villified and threatened "D'air Cunnial De Mur Sagart". "By the obligation of God as a Priest," he will have revenge, if it were to run for seven, ten, fifteen, or 21 years. . . .

10thly that old Anthony Burke who lives with his daughter and son in law in Muinnaba, and whose aged wife lived with another daughter in Claggeh—did upon the death of his wife offer 2^s/6^d to the Rev^d Mr. Conway to have mass said for the soul of his departed wife;—but that Mr. Conway not only refused the money but in a paroxysm of violence proclaimed Burke from the Altar, did ring the bell with rage—and invoke a horrible imprecation upon him and his worldly substance, for offering him 2^s/6^d to say Mass for the poor woman though no priest before Mr. Conway charged more than one shilling. The result was, that the Congregation would have slaughtered him ["him" crossed out] each other were it not for some peaceable characters who mollified the rage of the exasperated people. . . .

12thly we have had, through the pious zeal of Revd Neal McNulty, the walls of a good chapel 80 feet in length and 30 in breadth built for the last sixteen years, and not withstanding the number of clergymen that passed through this parish during that period, and collected great sums of money from us, for the ostensible purpose of roofing the Chapel, yet they have taken away our money and left us these sixteen years without a temple of worship to put our heads into or to screen us from the inclemency of the weather and although Dr Feeny has been appealed to against these clerical plunders, he has not ordered the money to be refunded to James O'Donel Esqr the Treasurer of our Chapel Committee.[19]

In order to sum up here, however, on the subject of clerical avarice, which is yet another subject, a long account of the situation in Ireland by T. Chisholme Anstey, an English Catholic, apparently to the secretary of Propaganda, Giovanni Brunelli, from London on November 17, 1843, is certainly worth our attention. In his account Anstey, who appears to have been well acquainted with the clergy and conditions in the province of Connaught, maintained, it is well known in every part of Ireland with which he is acquainted, and to the best of his belief also in other parts thereof, that however well disposed a parish priest or curate may be to relieve his parishioners or some of them from grievous and oppressive payments of the kinds specified ["Tithes, church dues, oblates, stock fees, money for repairs of fabric"], the relatives, (often very numerous) of such ecclesiastics are certain to obstruct the concession by clamorous complaints and remonstrances against his unkindness to his own flesh and blood, who by his ill timed liberality he is defrauding of their hopes of succession to his property after his death and of occasional contributions out of the same during his lifetime, and to which succession and contributions they in the popular opinion as well as in their own have a kind of equitable claim, founded upon the consent, which his family is supposed to have given in the first instance to his being withdrawn from field labor and domestic service in order to go to the seminary; and, that the fear of such complaints, remonstrances and appeals to popular opinion hath the effect of making the priests to be watchful and austere in the exact and undeviating levy of their aforesaid dues, is apparent from the greatness of their incomes; that is to say in Connaught, which is the cheapest part of Ireland, and where money is twice as valuable as it is in London, there are very few parish priests, if any, whose incomes are less than 200 sterling per annum although not one farthing of such incomes is appropriated by either priest or proper to any other purpose than the mere support of the priest. But in most parishes the income is very much higher and ranging to £500 and upwards per annum; insomuch that it is a vulgar and proverbial saying throughout Ireland that the best or richest matches are to be had with the kindred of priests and that their farms are certain to be well stocked and furnished.[20]

Anstey then went on to explain that there was a fixed tariff on burials, masses for the dead, churching women, etc., below which an offering might not fall, but might exceed it. Baptisms, he reported, were 2s. 6d., while marriages were a pound or a guinea, in addition to the money collected for the priest at the marriage feast. One such collection, Anstey noted, was £25, though no one there was above the rank of farmer. If the people involved were poor, Anstey admitted, the clergy would perform the required service gratis, but in order to test the truth of their allegations of poverty, the priests were in the habit of announcing in the chapel, church, or meeting house the names of those who had gratuitously received their services. "And, however poor the Irish peasant may be," he added, "he is rarely disposed to accept the exemption upon such humiliating conditions." The result of all of this had been, Anstey continued, that secret societies had been formed, and "by means of such associations they have from time to time endeavoured, and still are endeavouring, to compel the priests to agree to a more moderate tariff of dues and to compel the people to abstain from paying them any dues except according to the tariff appointed or proposed." Anstey then turned to the bad Irish habit of "stations," where the priest would designate the houses of various parishioners who were relatively well off as the place where he would hear confessions and say mass that week for all those in the immediate area. He complained that mass was being offered in "cabins" rather than in "chapels" because the fees were greater. The "station," moreover, he pointed out, was obliged to offer hospitality and had to cater to the priest's choice of tradesmen and victuallers. The Irish priests, Anstey further complained, not only did not keep to the rubric and practice of Rome in the Mass, but their sermons were of poor quality, and "the ignorance of the people in matters of Religion is frightful, and, in particular, that the doctrine of the Trinity is rarely known or ever heard of among them, much less the doctrine of the Real Presence and other articles of Faith." After all this and a good deal more Anstey finally concluded by advising the Propaganda that the only hope for religion in Ireland was for the pope to send a legate with power to correct the many abuses. Clerical avarice, however, legate or no, whether in terms of the clergy farming or grazing large tracts of land in their brothers's or nephews's names or in squeezing the people for alms and dues was, after drunkenness, the most difficult of the deadly sins for either the bishops or the laity to check.

But how many of the laity really cared? The best way to begin to answer that question is to determine how many people actually attended church. While it is certainly true that all those who attended mass religiously were not necessarily active in the concerns of their church, knowledge of the numbers who attended is at least helpful for setting an upper limit on those who were concerned. The figures on church attendance in pre-famine Ireland indicate that only thirty-three per cent of the Catholic population went to mass.[21] This is all the more remarkable in that in something less than fifty years church attendance would increase to over ninety per cent, and so it has continued down to the present day.[22] Why attendance was relatively so low in pre-famine Ireland is obvious. There were not enough priests and there were not enough churches, or, more particularly, not enough seating space in the existing churches to accommodate those who might be inclined to attend to their religious duties. If, for example, all the priests in Ireland celebrated the two masses they were allowed on a given Sunday in 1840 there would have been 4,300 masses for 6,500,000 people, or one mass for every 1,500 people in attendance, and there were no chapels and very few churches in pre-famine Ireland that would accommodate a thousand worshipers.

This deficiency was offset to some degree before the famine by the widespread practice of "stations." Baptism and marriage were also frequently celebrated in private houses rather than in churches. These practices were generally frowned on by those who were attempting to reform both clergy and laity and increase devotional zeal. The complaints of the reformers, who were concerned about the abuses attendant on the system, had mainly to do with the exorbitant "offerings" extracted by the clergy for the administration of the sacraments and the undignified if not unholy celebration of sacred rites in profane places. James Maher, writing from Carlow to his nephew Paul Cullen in Rome in early January 1842, asked "Could not Rome do something to stimulate the zeal and watchfulness of the Bishops: the holding of Stations for Mass and Confession at private houses is the very worst system. Wretched filthy cabins have been lately honored with stations." "The people," he explained,

> cannot be instructed. The Priest no matter how zealous cannot do his duty. The young clergyman is brought into contact with his female penitents. The result is confessions are often invalid or sacrilegious. It is almost impossible that the poor country people in the circumstances could disclose their sins. Struggling with their natural reluctance to avow their guilt, and fearing at the same time to be overheard by those who are pressing around the Priest, who cannot utter a word of encouragement to the sinner, except in the lowest and therefore intelligible [sic] whisper that can be expected.

"Could not Rome," Maher suggested again, "induce the Bishops to change the system? Stations in the chapels have been recommended in the Statutes for this province. But the recommendation has proved a dead letter." "We owe much to Rome," he assured Cullen in conclusion, "and if she would help us to this reform, we would be more deeply her debtor."[23] Nearly all the synods, provincial and national, between 1830 and 1875 had statutes disapproving of "stations," and even though Rome eventually added her proscription as requested by Father Maher, the practice died very hard, especially in the south and west where it still survives in some places.[24]

Before the famine, then, despite severe limitations in plant and personnel, there was a small but perceptible change and increase in devotional practices in Ireland. Why this was so had a great deal to do with the enthusiasm and hope generated by the moral and political reform movements of Father Mathew and Daniel O'Connell. Both the Total Abstinence Society and the Repeal Association grew up in a period heavy with gloomy forebodings of impending disaster as bad harvest succeeded bad harvest, prices for foodstuffs continued to fall rapidly, and emigration mounted. Literally millions took Father Mathew's temperance pledge as the production of Irish whisky fell from 12,296,000 gallons in 1839 to 5,546,283 gallons in 1844. As Daniel O'Connell enrolled the "nation" in his Repeal Association his "monster meetings" numbered in the hundreds of thousands of people.[25] Essentially these were both revival movements, which created not only an enormous enthusiasm but, because of the underlying anxieties created by population pressure and land hunger, also contributed greatly to an already heavily charged emotional atmosphere. In the early 1840s, therefore, there already were manifest signs of that devotional revolution, which Paul Cullen would proceed to help make and consolidate some ten years later when he would arrive in Ireland as archbishop of Armagh and apostolic delegate.

On the occasion of a papal jubilee in 1842, for example, when the penitents were offered special indulgences if they would but confess their sins and come to Christ, the bishop of Cork wrote to Cullen in Rome asking the rector of the Irish College to secure for him additional faculties to dispense in terms of sins especially reserved to the pope. "Sinners," John Murphy explained to Cullen in May 1842, "who have for years lived in fornication, adultery, incest & have recourse to the tribunal of penance" are coming in in droves. "I have a melancholy list of 64 couples," he added sadly,

who in obedience to my commands have separated *a thora*; for where there is abject poverty, with a numerous brood we cannot insist on separation *a mensa*. The Jubilee is open in only one Parish, how numerous will be the blacklist before the conclusion of it in the whole diocese—it would be endless to enter into the minute details of every case.[26]

Some nine months later James Maher again reported to his nephew in Rome from Carlow. "I forgot, tho I intended it to tell you of the wonderful success of the Missionaries in Athy." "A visit from Father Mathew," he explained, "would not have put a greater number in motion. Hundreds remained all night in the Chapel, and many remained in town away from their homes from 5 and six days waiting an opportunity of confessing." "This extraordinary movement," Maher further noted, "has confirmed an old opinion of mine that we do not always afford the people an opportunity of general confession when required. In fact we have not half Priests for the wants of the Mission, and a very considerable proportion of the Parrochi leave the confessional almost entirely to the curates." The following August Cullen's sister Margaret informed him that they had had the "Missioners" in Carlow town for the last five weeks, and that it "would be impossible for me to describe the enthusiasm of the people." If the missioners were angels from heaven, she added, they could not be more venerated. Work was at a standstill, while people followed them around all day and crowded "in *hundreds* to the Confessionals, many very many who had never before been there." The missioners preached three times a day in the chapel, which was "crowded to suffocation." "What a pity," she finally concluded, "we have not more Priests in the Parish. I fear a great deal of their labours will go for nothing. Where is the opportunity for the *bulk* of the parish to approach the Holy sacraments."[27]

Indeed, the "bulk" of the Irish people in the 1840s never did have the opportunity to approach the sacraments. In writing his customary annual letter in October 1851 to the cardinal prefect of Propaganda, for example, Michael Jones, a former student of the Propaganda's Urban College in Rome, complained about "an almost general neglect in giving the People the necessary knowledge of the Faith, the Commandments and the Sacraments." "The Irish People," Jones explained to Cardinal Fransoni, "are very good, but much neglected in every way by both the Civil and Ecclesiastical Government, more by the latter than the former." It was time "for the Ecclesiastical authority to put an end to the present state of things." The priests who received training at the National Seminary at Maynooth, did "not receive in the College any notion how things should be. The old system of the days of Persecution, the Catacombs, and the Caves is all that they know."[28] That the Irish people were receptive and might have made excellent evangelical material to work with is certainly given credence by the unusual success of the sporadic attempts made, but the resources available for a religious and moral revival on a national scale were too slender in the face of the number of people.

What achievement there was before the famine, then, was largely confined to that "respectable" class of Catholics, typified by the Cullens and the Mahers in Carlow, who were economically better off. Since this class generally survived the famine intact, while the "bulk" of the cottiers, laborers, and paupers were swept away by starvation, disease, and emigration, the Church actually had a stronger devotional nucleus relative to absolute numbers in 1850 than in 1840.[29] This nucleus, furthermore, would come to count for more with every succeeding year because the remaining subsistence population was gradually liquidated by a continuing emigration sparked periodically by the fear of starvation. When Paul Cullen arrived in Ireland he therefore had a potentially more favorable situation than has been generally supposed. He also patently derived very great advantage from the psychological impact the famine had on those who remained in Ireland. The growing awareness of a sense of sin already apparent in the 1840s was certainly deepened as God's wrath was made manifest in a great natural disaster that destroyed and scattered his people. Psychologically and socially, therefore, the Irish people were ready for a great evangelical revival, while economically and organizationally the Church was now correspondingly ready after the famine to meet their religious and emotional needs.

The problem of characterizing the making and consolidating of this devotional revolution is somewhat simplified by the fact that the period begins with the first National Synod of Thurles in 1850 and ends with the second National Synod of Maynooth in 1875. The first Synod of Thurles was primarily concerned with the proper administraiton of the sacraments and regulating more closely the lives of the parish clergy.[30] In the statutes the clergy were exhorted to administer the sacraments more often and only in church, except where it was impossible, and to encourage the laity to better lives by the clergy's own good example. The bishops were assigned the responsibility by the synod of seeing that these reforms were carried out in their respective dioceses. Twenty-five years later the Synod of Maynooth reiterated mainly what had already been decreed in 1850 and in enlarging upon the statutes further increased episcopal control and authority.[31] The making of the law, however, proved to be one thing, and the enforcing of it quite another. The first Synod of Thurles had made it quite clear that the Church was to be reformed from the top down and that the responsibility for enforcing that reform should fall to the bishops. As apostolic delegate, however, Cullen had very real difficulties in keeping the Irish bishops up to the mark. The problem was not only that a large number of bishops were set in their ways and naturally averse to reform, but that the bishops also had serious differences with regard to educational and political matters, and their quarrels in these areas seriously inhibited their efforts at pastoral reform.

Cullen, however, was not only a reformer but a very effective ecclesiastical politician, and with the support of Rome, especially in episcopal appointments, the Irish Church was reformed by him in his generation. His method was to deal with one principal issue at a time, while trying to contain the worst effects of the other issues. His fellow archbishops of Dublin, Tuam, and Cashel, for example, each respectively represented educatinal, political, and pastoral problems for Cullen. He mobilized Tuam and Cashel against the educational policies concerning the Queen's Colleges, advocated by the venerable archbishop of Dublin, Daniel Murray, who was strongly supported by a minority of the bishops. When Murray died in the winter of 1852 Cullen was translated by Rome from Armagh to Dublin and his nominee appointed to replace him in Armagh. The opposition among the bishops, without the effective leadership of Murray, was quickly isolated and eventually crushed. Cullen then turned to the problem posed by the archbishop of Tuam, John MacHale, and the involvement of the clergy in secular politics, particularly the Tenant League. Supported by Armagh and Cashel, and with Rome's aid, MacHale was also eventually isolated, and if not crushed, he was at least effectively contained. Finally Cullen tackled the problem of pastoral reform in the province of Cashel, which was most difficult because most of the bishops of that province strongly supported the custom of "stations." Cullen once again undermined the opposition to him by having only those who agreed with his reform principles succeed to bishoprics in that province, and gradually but relentlessly those bishops who were reluctant to change their ways in the rest of Ireland were replaced by Cullen's more energetic and aggressive nominees. By 1875, therefore, there was hardly a bishop in Ireland, except MacHale, who did not zealously promote pastoral reform in his diocese, whatever his educational and political views were. Actually this

Now ready, strongly bound, 426 pp. 18mo, with Imprimatur of the Lord Bishop of Kildare, 1s.,

THE

PEOPLE'S PRAYER BOOK,

WITH

SHORT SIMPLE INSTRUCTIONS

ON THE

VARIOUS DUTIES OF RELIGION,

AND

AN EASY CATECHISM

For the use of Adults whose religious instruction had been neglected.

By REV. THOMAS MURPHY, P.P.,

MOUNTMELLICK.

☞ In concurrence with the desire of the Rev. Mr. Murphy there will be a considerable reduction made to those who purchase for distribution amongst the poor and uninstructed.

A neat and beautiful Edition of the above "Invaluable Prayer Book," in superior binding, may be had from the Publisher.

DUBLIN :

JOHN MULLANY, 1 PARLIAMENT-STREET.

1873.

From the *Irish Catholic Directory, 1873* (Dublin, 1873).

RELIGIOUS ARTICLES

FOR

CATHOLIC CHURCHES, COMMUNITIES, CONVENTS, &c.

MAISON FRANCAISE

(*French House*).

OFFICES:

7 WELLINGTON QUAY,	**12 Rue Duguay Trouin,**
DUBLIN,	**PARIS,**
Near Essex Bridge.	*Near St. Sulpice's Church.*

MONSIEUR L. GUERET,

Publisher and Manufacturer in Paris.

RESPECTFULLY begs to inform the Roman Catholic Clergy, Heads of Religious Houses, Convents, &c., that he is able to offer them a large and selected stock of Religious Goods, such as Lace Pictures for Prayer-books; Beautiful Emblems, embroidered on rice paper, and others printed; Pictures in Sheets, New Chromos in Sheets, large plain, coloured and black ground Pictures of all kinds of subjects, with or without frames. Sheets of Hearts, red, blue, and purple; small and large Stations of the Cross in Oil Paintings, also in plain; coloured and black ground Engravings framed. Mortuary Cards in Sheets, or printed by hundred or half hundred. Scapulars; Standing Lamps of every colour; Branches for Benediction, with 3, 5, 7, 12 lights. The best Incense of Jerusalem, guaranteed to be of the same quality used in Rome and all the Churches on the Continent. Brass and Silver Beads and Medals; Pearl Crosses and Medals for School Distribution, Pictures, Medals, and Statues of Our Lady of Lourdes. Handsome Crucifixes, coppered, bronzed, and gilt, also in plastic and Ivory; Irish Lockets, and sets of Green Enamelled Shamrocks. Altar Lights; Cruets; Ornamental Chapels in carved wood for private Oratories; Holy-water Fonts; Glass Shades; Large Statues in plaster and terra-cotta; Small Statues in French plastic and biscuit; Vases for Natural and Artificial Flowers; Candlesticks in bronze and silvered glass; Cribs in plaster and plastic of every size and price. Infant Jesus in Wax; Hearts, Crowns, and Monograms; Articles of Paris for Bazaars.

N.B.—Orders by Post punctually executed, and forwarded to any part of Ireland *carriage free, when amounting to £6.* Large Statues and Heavy Bronzes excepted.

☞ Special prices for the Clergy and Religious Communities.

WHOLESALE AND RETAIL,

7 WELLINGTON QUAY, 7
Near Essex Bridge.

From the *Irish Catholic Directory, 1873* (Dublin, 1873).

THE APPARITION AT KNOCK Cᵒ MAYO.

AS SEEN ON AUGT 21ST 1879.   EVE OF THE OCTAVE OF THE ASSUMPTION.

MANY MIRACULOUS CURES HAVE BEEN EFFECTED THERE SINCE THE ABOVE OCCURRENCE.

THIS VIEW WAS TAKEN ON THE SPOT BY W.COLLINS.

AND SUBMITTED TO, AND APPROVED OF BY THE SEVERAL PERSONS WHO SAW THE ABOVE

About 7:30 on the evening of the 21st of August, 1879, the vigil of the octave day of the Feast of the Assumption at the parish church of Knock, Co. Mayo, "an apparition of Our Blessed Lady, wearing a large brilliant crown and clothes in white garments was distinctly seen by some fifteen persons at the south gable wall of the church. Our Lady is described as having her hands raised as if in prayer and her eyes turned towards heaven. On her right hand was St. Joseph, his head inclined towards her, and on her left was St. John the Evangelist, attired as a bishop, his left hand holding a book and his right hand raised as if in preaching. To the left of St. John was an altar on which stood a cross and a Lamb, about 8 weeks old. . . . The gable wall where this manifestation was seen was covered with a cloud of light and the vision lasted for fully two hours." Liam Ua Cadain, *Venerable Arch-Deacon Cavanagh, Pastor of Knock, 1867–1897* (Dublin, 1955), 69. Illustration courtesy of National Library of Ireland.

resoltuion of the distribution of power in the Irish Church in favor of Cullen was not nearly as smooth or inevitable as it may appear from this oversimplified account, but what is most important to understand is that this resolution of power was absolutely necessary to the making and consolidation of the devotional revolution that took place.

In the twenty years following Cullen's arrival in Ireland the number of priests was increased by some seven hundred, or nearly twenty-five per cent, to a total of about 3,200, while the Catholic population declined from five to four million, or a ratio increase of one priest to 2,000 people to one priest to 1,250 people in 1870. The nun population increased even more rapidly over the same period. In 1850, for example, there were only some 1,500 nuns in Ireland, while in 1870 there were more than 3,700 or an absolute increase of 2,200, and a ratio increase of 1 : 3,300 in 1850 to 1 : 1,100 in 1870.[32] Not only were the numbers of clergy relative to the population rapidly appreciating, but it also appears that their quality was improving over the same period. The amount of dirty clerical linen washed in Rome appears to have decreased, as did the volume of litigation between the bishops and their priests. The improving quality of the clergy, moreover, is not only testified to by their really prodigious energy in building churches, schools, seminaries, convents, and parochial houses, but their conduct and learning was certainly improved by conferences, retreats, synods, and the erection of cathedral chapters, as well as by the annual or triennial visitations by their bishops depending on the size of their dioceses.

In extending their increasing zeal and piety to the laity the clergy centered their attention on the sacraments, and especially on the sacraments of penance and Holy Eucharist. Confession and communion, which usually had been associated with a practicing Catholic's Easter duty in pre-famine Ireland, now became much more frequent. To encourage the laity, missions were held in nearly every parish in Ireland in the decade of the fifties. Pastoral gains thus made were consolidated by the introduction of a whole series of devotional exercises designed not only to encourage more frequent participation in the sacraments but to instill veneration by an appreciation of their ritual beauty and intrinsic mystery. The spiritual rewards, of course, for these devotional exercises were the various indulgences, which shortened either the sinner's or the sinner's loved one's time of torment in purgatory. The new devotions were mainly of Roman origin and included the rosary, forty hours, perpetual adoration, novenas, blessed altars, *Via Crucis,* benediction, vespers, devotion to the Sacred Heart and to the Immaculate Conception, jubilees, triduums, pilgrimages, shrines, processions, and retreats. These devotional exercises, moreover, were organized in order to communalize and regularize practice under a spiritual director and included sodalities, confraternities such as the various purgatorian societies, the Society of St. Vincent de Paul, and Peter's Pence as well as temperance and altar societies. These public exercises were also reinforced by the use of devotional tools and aids: beads, scapulars, medals, missals, prayer books, catechisms, holy pictures, and *Agnus Dei,* all blessed by priests who had recently acquired that privilege from Rome through the intercession of their bishops. Furthermore, this was the period when the whole world of the senses was explored in these devotional exercises, and especially in the Mass, through music, singing, candles, vestments, and incense.

The evidence in support of this vast social change, of course, is too diversified and complicated to be presented coherently here. Still, in order to acquire perhaps at least the flavor of that phenomenon, if not its extent, it might be useful to follow selectively the career of the man who spearheaded that change in the initial years. "I was in Armagh," Cullen reported shortly after his arrival in Ireland to Tobias Kirby in Rome, "and saw nearly all the clergy." "The old Cathedral," he explained, obviously scandalized, "is awfully bad—the priests use only *one* tallow candle on the altars at mass in the Cathedral. Imagine what it must be elsewhere." Three months later Laurence Forde, Cullen's master of ceremonies at the Synod of Thurles, reported to Kirby that the opening day's solemnities were a grand Roman success with high mass being celebrated *alla* Palestrina, complete with assistant priest, deacon, and subdeacons. "I gave the seventh candlestick," Forde assured Kirby,

to Dr. Cullen at the Mass. I was not quite certain if it should be so, but I acted on your advice. It is not without its effect—I think it useful to go in some things even a little beyond strict practice for the sake of letting the bishops and clergy see the full solemnities of the Church.[33]

Some two years later, when he had been translated to Dublin, the richest and most influential diocese in Ireland, Cullen still was concerned about setting the proper tone. "We commenced the Jubilee here yesterday," he reported to Kirby in October 1852, "I *sang* more meo high mass attended by all the Chapter and dignitaries of Dublin." Mr. Faber, the celebrated English priest, "preached a magnificent sermon by far the most eloquent I ever heard," giving "a new tone and a Catholic one to Dublin." "We have the *40 ore*," he noted further, referring to his pro-Cathedral, "at Marlboro St. with great pomp and magnificence. The Church is ornamented with damask, a great machine erected and what is better crowds of people are attending. Deo Gratias. The devotion will be continued through the entire three months of the jubilee." He finally assured Kirby in Italian that he would soon see "the fruits of our preaching." Two months later, on December 8, in a letter headed "Evviva Maria," Cullen again reported to Kirby that the jubilee, the forty hours, and the novena in process were all very successful. "Here," he added even more significantly, "we are trying to enrol a large missionary body before next summer to wipe out the proselytizers everywhere." "It is necessary to see," Cullen concluded prudently in Italian, "if it will be successful, and then I will write to Propaganda. The Jesuits, Dominicans, Carmelites, Vincentians, Redemptorists, secular Priests will all join together—but."[34]

"The Jubilee," Cullen again assured Kirby less than two weeks later, on December 20, 1852, "has succeeded beyond all hope. All the churches are crowded with people trying to go to confession. Were the priests ten times as many as they are they could not hear them all." "I have done nothing lately," he added, breaking into Italian,

> but to cure invalid marriages and remedy similar impediments. We must beg of the Pope to give a Jubilee of one month next May. It will put down all heresies—and set things right. . . . The priests are greatly fatigued with the Jubilee otherwise I w^d apply at present to have it prolonged.

"Some of the people here," Cullen then noted, indicating that devotional practices were becoming contagious, "are anxious I should establish in the schools and convents the 'Child of Mary' such as they have in Waterford convent. Will you get me faculties to do this, and to establish every other sodality. I w^d require to know what the indulgences are and what the rules."[35]

Early in the new year Cullen again wrote Kirby complaining that all was not well in the various parts of the Irish Church. "I wrote some days ago to Propaganda regarding the diocese of Ardagh," he explained in Italian in January 1853. "It seems to me," Cullen noted, "that it would be well to appoint a bishop quickly." "Father John Kilduff," he suggested, referring to a Vincentian on the Dublin mission, "a native of the diocese would be the saving of it." "He is a good preacher," Cullen continued, giving an interesting example of what he thought was important in a bishop, "a good theologian, full of zeal, and yet courageous enough. Such a man would be required to reform the diocese. He is about 33 years of age." "In the diocese of Cashel," Cullen then informed Kirby, turning to another trouble spot, "there is a parish called Doon, where I have heard there are seven or eight hundred apostates." "The Archbishop of Cashel, however," he reported, "does not want any noise made about it. Father Dowley, Superior of the Vincentians recently offered to give a mission but so far the offer has not been acknowledged." "The poor Archbishop," he added, "is very timid, and believes that he is always on the verge of death, even though he is in good health." "He is almost the only bishop," Cullen complained, "that has done nothing about what was prescribed in the Synod of Thurles." "Baptisms and confessions remain as they formerly were, and they also celebrate marriages in private houses. In almost all the other dioceses something at least has been done." "In this diocese of Dublin," he then explained,

> all marriages and baptisms are celebrated in the churches. In the city and in the towns all the confessions are heard in the churches. In all the mountainous places where there are no churches nearby, if the distance is not too great, I told the priest to find every means of transporting the people to those distant churches—but if that were not possible to hear the confessions in private houses (except in case of illness), if the church is not more than two miles away.[36]

"Evviva S. Patrizio," Cullen greeted Kirby again some two months later on March 17, 1853, and continued in Italian, "I have already convened a provincial synod to be held in Dublin at Pentecost. The Bishops are not pleased." "Now it is necessary to see," Cullen explained, "quid agendum. There are things enough to be done— but it is difficult to put them in order and I must do all myself. There is no one who knows how to draw up a decree or write a line of Latin." "Monsignor Dixon," Cullen then reported, referring to the new archbishop of Armagh, "has already visited Ardagh and has promised to write in favor of Kilduff." It is Kilduff, Cullen added tenaciously in conclusion, who would be "the salvation of that unfortunate diocese."[37] Kilduff "will be consecrated here by me on S. Peters day." Dr. Dawson, the popular candidate among the Ardagh priests, "has written him a most foolishly impolite letter, which shows he was never fit to be a Bishop." Every attempt had been made "to get up some agitation against Kilduff by Dawsons friends—protests I believe have been sent to Rome—but the people are delighted, and the greatest part of the clergy—the appointment was absolutely necessary." "I have been told," Cullen added, referring to the archbishop of Tuam and the bishop of Clogher, "that Dr. McHale and Dr. McNally spoke against it—but this is only a report." "There is no doubt however," he assured Kirby again, "that K. [Kilduff] will be a blessing to the diocese—tho' he will have to carry his cross with the opp. of Dawson & Co." "I send you the acts and decrees of the Council in a day or two with a letter to the Pope," Cullen then noted, referring to his recently concluded provincial synod. "In Cashel," he then complained again of the archbishop, "I hear, Dr. Slattery has not made a single change as yet. Marriages, baptisms, confessions still, as formerly in private houses. The same in several dioceses and I believe in Tuam." "It will be necessary," he advised darkly, "to do something in these matters." "But," he concluded characteristically, and appropriately breaking into Italian, "little by little all will be accomplished."[38]

This brief account of Cullen's early attempt at reforming the Irish Church in the interests of making and consolidating a devotional revolution is useful as a model, though a somewhat imperfect one, of his own continuing attempts, and those of his protégés, at reform over the next twenty-five years. In general Cullen preferred to promote men like Kilduff who were made in his own image and likeness. They were not only good preachers, adequate theologians, zealous, courageous enough, and young, but they were also generally strangers to the diocese and, therefore, they did not have any of the personal ties or loyalties that might inhibit them in their zeal for reform. If they were not recruited from the regular clergy, moreover, the new bishops were usually rectors or vice-rectors of seminaries—strict, stern, austere men who had both the experience of, and a proven talent for, efficient administration. They were also well aware that the new discipline they represented would not be popular among their priests, but if these bishops were ever to make their wills effective with their clergy, the bishops would have to depend on their patron's continued exertions on their behalf at

Rome. They all tended, therefore, to be ultramontanes, because Rome was not only the theoretical but the actual source of their own and Cullen's real power in the Irish Church.

While all of the foregoing may tell one something about what this devotional revolution consisted of and, at least partially, how it was made, the crucial question still remains—why did the Irish people respond so readily to the reform of their Church and become virtually practicing Catholics within a generation? The Great Famine was truly a gigantic psychological shock, and it certainly would be both neat and convenient to be able to assign so impressive a cause for so remarkable an effect. A guilt-ridden and frightened people turning more formally and fervently to their God in their hour of need makes more, indeed, than a good deal of superficial sense. The problem, of course, is that the devotional need appears to have been increasingly present before the famine, and only the adverse circumstances of population growth and the lack of money and personnel on the part of the Church prevented that need from being realized. The famine, therefore, was as much the occasion for as it was a cause of the devotional revolution being made and consolidated in Ireland, and one must probe more deeply if one is to understand why as well as how this remarkable historical phenomenon took place.

What I would like to suggest is that the devotional revolution which took place after the famine satisfied more than the negative factors of guilt and fear induced by that great catastrophe. There may indeed be something worse than the simple fear of being destroyed—the mounting terror in the growing awareness that one is being destroyed. The Irish, after all, had been gradually losing their language, their culture, and their way of life for nearly a hundred years before the famine. Education, business, politics, and communication in the written word, even more than in the spoken word, were all increasingly geared to English as the Irish were being effectively Anglicized, or, perhaps more appropriately, West Britonized. There has been so much concern, for example, in the study of Irish history in the nineteenth century with the geography of emigration that it has hardly been noticed that the Irish before the famine had nearly all become cultural emigrants, that they had in fact moved in their minds before a good many of them had actually to move in space.[39] In a word, then, Irishmen who were aware of being Irish were losing their identity, and this accounts in large part for their becoming practicing Catholics. The devotional revolution, I would argue further, provided the Irish with a substitute symbolic language and offered them a new cultural heritage with which they could identify and be identified and through which they could identify with one another. This is why, for example, Irish and Catholic have become almost interchangeable terms in Ireland, despite the attempts of Nationalists to make Irish rather than Catholic the inclusive term. "Take an average Irishman," the celebrated Irish Dominican preacher, Father Tom Burke, said in 1872, "—I don't care where you find him—and you will find that the very first principle in his mind is, 'I am not an Englishman, because I am a Catholic! Take an Irishman wherever he is found, all over the earth, and any casual observer will at once come to the conclusion, 'Oh; he is an Irishman, he is a Catholic!' The two go together."[40]

Finally it is necessary to observe that the making and consolidating of this devotional revolution had a wider and deeper significance than even making practicing Catholics of the Irish people in a generation. One can argue that the cause and effect relationship between what may be popularly called in the best current sociological jargon a group "identity crisis," and the resolution of it in what was fundamentally a religious revival has some very serious implications for, as well as allowing for some very interesting insights into, the history of the Irish people both at home and abroad in the nineteenth century. Daniel O'Connell, for example, if viewed as the bridge between the old and the new Ireland rather than as the divide between Old and Young Ireland, becomes not only more important but more understandable as the great transitional figure in modern Irish history.[41] Further, the devotional revolution and its general and particular causes are crucial to understanding the development of Irish nationalism and the cultural importance of Irish Catholicism in that development.[42] Moreover, the cultural revivals of Young Ireland in the middle of the century and the Gaelic movement at the end appear less ludicrous in the light of the identity crisis that had been taking place since the turn of the century, and Daniel Corkery and the other archpriests of the language movement in more recent times may indeed yet come into their own.[43]

Last but not least in this necessarily less than complete catalog of what was significant in the devotional revolution is its importance for understanding the great Diaspora of the Irish people in the nineteenth century, as more than four million of them found new homes in a new world. Most of the two million Irish who emigrated between 1847 and 1860 were part of the pre-famine generation of nonpracticing Catholics, if indeed they were Catholics at all. They congregated in the ghettos of English, American, and Canadian cities where they acquired a fearful reputation for ignorance, drunkenness, vice, and violence. What the famine Irish actually represented, therefore, was a culture of poverty that had been in the making in Ireland since the late eighteenth century because of the pressure of population on the means of subsistence. That culture produced all the circumstances and most of the values that the British and the Americans were to find most repugnant in the Irish. The crucial point here, however, is that after the famine that culture of poverty was broken up in Ireland by emigration, and the new circumstances created by that breakup allowed for the emergence of other values.

Of the four million Irish, for example, who immigrated to the United States between 1845 and 1900, some 2,300,000 came after 1860. By 1860 there already were in Ireland 3,000 priests and 2,600 nuns for a Catholic population of 4,500,000, or one priest for every 1,500 people and one nun for every 1,700. In 1900 there were 3,700 priests and 8,000 nuns for a further reduced Catholic population of 3,300,000, or a ratio of one priest for every 900 and one nun for about every 400 people.[44] Besides this remarkable improvement in the clerical population vis-à-vis the Catholic population in Ireland, the Irish Church during this period exported a very large number of priests and nuns to help staff churches in the United States and the rest of the English-speaking world.[45] What these crude figures suggest is that the Irish were transformed as a people—men and women alike—into practicing Catholics. The succeeding waves of these recently created devotional Catholics brought their cultural and religious needs and corresponding values with them when they emigrated, and in doing so they helped to reclaim those lapsed and nonpracticing "shanty" Irish. The newer, "lace-curtain" Irish found it progressively easier to assimilate to their new environment, because they were objectively less objectionable.

In a word, then, the Irish immigrants in this country in 1900 were a vast improvement over the generation of famine Irish who had arrived before 1860, and that improvement was not evident simply in terms of social behavior. Not only were later immigrants less drunken and less prone to violence, they also had acquired basic educational skills and were actually less poor. Average daily attendance in the Irish National System of Education increased from 100,000 in 1840 to nearly 500,00 in 1900, and this in spite of the fact that the population had been reduced by one-half over that period of time.[46] The literacy figures reveal that in 1861 45.8 per cent of Roman Catholics were unable to read and write, but by 1901 the figure had dropped to 16.4 per cent, a decline that was reflected in comparative literacy figures for various immigrant groups in the United States after the turn of the century.[47] Economic conditions in Ireland, furthermore, improved between 1840 and 1900, though the economy was certainly a very sick one, and the culture of poverty that was broken at the famine was liquidated partly by that improvement and partly by the continuing emigration, leaving the remaining population relatively less poor. No factor, then, was more important in the moral and social improvement of the Irish people either at home or abroad in the nineteenth century than the devotional revolution between 1850 and 1875; yet no aspect of recent Irish history has received less attention.

NOTES

[1] J. P. Cooke to Kirby, Kirby Papers, Archives of the Irish College, Rome.

[2] Dec. 19, 1877, Kirby Papers.

[3] Emmet Larkin, "Church and State in Ireland in the Nineteenth Century," *Church History*, 31 (1962): 295–306.

[4] Emmet Larkin, "Economic Growth, Capital Investment, and the Roman Catholic Church in Nineteenth Century Ireland," *AHR*, 72 (1966–67): 852–84.

[5] Charles Vane, marquess of Londonderry, ed., *Memoirs and Correspondence of Viscount Castlereagh*, 4: 99, 172.

[6] *Census of Ireland, 1851* (Dublin, 1856).

[7] "First Report of the Commissioners of Public Instruction, Ireland," *Parliamentary Papers*, 1835, vol. 33, no. 45. The estimate of the Catholic population is based on the percentages of the various denominations given in this first religious census taken in Ireland in 1834: Population (total) 7,943,940; Catholic 6,427,712; Church of Ireland 852,064; Presbyterian 642,356; Other 21,808. According to these figures the Catholics made up nearly 81 per cent of the total population, while the combined Protestant total was about 19 per cent. If, therefore, the Catholic population in 1841 is estimated at 80 per cent of the census figure of 8,175,000 for the total population, the round number of Catholics is about 6,500,000. The Catholic populations of 3,900,000 in 1800 and 5,250,000 in 1850 are also based on taking 80 per cent of an estimated total in 1800 and a census total in 1851 respectively of 4,900,000 and 6,554,074, though both in 1800 and 1850 the percentage of Protestants to Catholics was more likely to have been somewhat higher than in 1834, the probable peak year of the Catholic population bulge in the first half of the nineteenth century. In 1861, for example, when for the first time the decennial census included figures for

religious denominations, the Catholics accounted for some 78 per cent of the total population.

[8] *Census of Ireland, 1851.*

[9] *Census of Ireland, 1841* (Dublin, 1843).

[10] *Scritture riferite nei congressi, Irlanda*, 18, fol. 316.

[11] *Ibid.*, 20, fol. 69.

[12] *Ibid.*, 21, fols. 158–59.

[13] A critical bibliography of the numerous pious lives of Irish bishops, priests, monks, and nuns is also beyond the scope of this article. An honorable exception to this general charge of hagiography, however, must be noted in W. J. Fitz-Patrick's very fine Victorian, two-volume biography, *The Life, Times and Correspondence of the Right Rev. Dr. Doyle, Bishop of Kildare and Leighlin* (Dublin, 1880). In setting a lower limit in this biographical spectrum, the best example is perhaps Peader MacSuibhne's more recent three-volume effort, *Paul Cullen and His Contemporaries* (Naas, 1961–65). For a partial list, at least of those biographies that range between the upper and lower limits set above, see the bibliography in T. J. Walsh, *Nano Nagle and the Presentation Sisters* (Dublin, 1959).

[14] The milestone in effecting the better conduct of the clergy by increasing the authority of the bishops was the simultaneous holding of diocesan synods in the four dioceses that made up the province of Dublin in the third week of July 1831. For an account of the background to the meetings, see William Meagher, *Notices of the Life and Character of His Grace, Most Rev. Daniel Murray, Late Archbishop of Dublin* (Dublin, 1853), 128–31; for the legislation of synods, see R. T. McGhee, *Diocesan Statutes of the Roman Catholic Bishops of the Province of Leinster* (London, 1837); for an excellent account of a reforming bishop, James Doyle (1819–34), see Fitz-Patrick, *Life, Times,* 1: 101–32.

[15] Meagher, *Notices,* 11–12.

[16] "Report from the Lords Committees appointed a secret committee to enquire into the State of Ireland," 1825, *PP*, vol. 7, no. 521, pt. 2, Minutes of Evidence, p. 569. Mortimer O'Sullivan, a Church of Ireland clergyman, was asked, "Are you acquainted with the early habits of life, of persons who afterwards become Roman Catholics priests?—Yes. / From what class of life are they generally taken?—I think generally speaking from the lower orders. My connection with an endowed school, gave me an opportunity of knowing more particularly. / Of course you have been acquainted with some who have afterwards gone to Maynooth?—Yes. / Have you had any occasion to observe what have been the effects of a collegiate education upon those persons?—It appeared to me to leave them, with respect to their moral qualities and their political prejudices, just what they were before they had gone there. When I speak of the lower orders, I mean the poorer classes; there are some of a higher order; and that church shows great judgement in disposing of her clergy; those of better manners and better information are generally placed in the towns: and those persons who are from their habits and from their education less fitted to appear in public, are left in the country parts."

[17] The problem of exorbitant clerical dues and the resistance of the laity to them had been an issue in Ireland from at least the latter part of the eighteenth century. See Robert E. Burns, "Parson, Priests, and the People: The Rise of Irish Anti-Clericalism, 1785–89," *Church History,* 31 (1962): 151–63.

[18] McGhee, *Diocesan Statutes,* xli–xlii.

[19] *Scritture riferite nei congressi, Irlanda*, 28, fols. 634–35. The petition is signed by James O'Donel as "Chairman of the Parochial Committee" and Hugh Joseph O'Donel as "Secretary." Three other petitioners signed their names, but nineteen others made their "X" mark and were signed for.

[20] *Ibid.*, fols. 121–45.

[21] David W. Miller, "Religion and Social Change in Pre-Famine Ireland," unpublished paper, p. 3. Since the writing of his paper Professor Miller has revised his estimate of church attendance by Roman Catholics upward to about 40 per cent, but he is still "prepared to state flatly that the prevalence of extraordinary religious devotion evidenced by extremely regular church attendance is a post-Famine phenomenon."

[22] Jean Blanchard, *The Church in Contemporary Ireland* (Dublin, 1963), 29–31.

[23] Jan. 2, 1842, Cullen Papers, Archives of the Irish College, Rome.

[24] Blanchard, *Church in Contemporary Ireland*, 32.

[25] Sir James O'Connor, *History of Ireland, 1798–1924* (London, 1925), 1: 301; L. J. McCaffrey, *Daniel O'Connell and the Repeal Year* (Lexington, 1966).

[26] May 29, 1842, Cullen Papers.

[27] Feb. 21, Aug. 30, 1843, Ibid.

[28] Michele Jones to Giacomo Cardinale Fransoni, Oct. 9, 1851, *Scritture riferite nei congressi, Irlanda,* 30, fols. 720–21, Archives of the Society for the Propagation of the Faith, Rome. The original letter is in Italian. See also K., Feb. 28, 1858, for a letter from John Kyne, chaplain at Alum Bagh, Lucknow, Oude, East India, to Thomas Grant, bishop of Southwark (London) and Catholic chaplain-general, regarding Kyne's work among the British troops, who were mainly Irish and presumably Catholic. "I am anxious first of all to communicate to your Lordship the pleasing fact that even here in India I can bear testimony from personal experience, to the good effect produced by the Mission given last year to the soldiers at Chatham. In fact the recruits, who arrived here last month from Chatham are the *only* persons of whom it can be said, that they complied with the Easter obligation. With this exception, the rest of the poor soldiers were in a most pitiable state. The vast majority had never in their lives received the Holy Sacraments. And their ignorance of even the first principles of religion was truly astonishing with all my experience I was never in my life so taken by surprize. If I had heard it from others, I could not have believed it possible. Yet with all that they are not bad materials to work upon—I believe, notwithstanding the general impression to the contrary, that on the whole as much may be made of them as of any other class of Christians." By way of proof Kyne explained that in three months he had brought upward of a thousand to the sacraments and that every morning he had between thirty to fifty communicants, while every evening he recited the rosary and gave religious instruction.

[29] John Kepple to Kirby, Sept. 2, 1852, Kirby Papers. Writing from Ballyhea, Charleville, where he was parish priest, Kepple noted, "There is not in the County of Cork a finer country than this. The population of my parish is not very large, the poorer portion of it (as everywhere else through out Ireland) has been swept away by the Famine fever emigration &c &c. The farmers tho' not numerous are very respectable, and comfortable but in consequence of the failure of crops, and the thinness of the people our emoluments here are inconsiderable, however I don't complain."

[30] *Decreta, Synodi Nationalis Totius Hiberniae Thurlesiae Habitae Anno MDCCCL* (Dublin, 1851).

[31] *Decreta, Synodi Plenariae Episcoporum Hiberniae, Habitae Apud Maynutium, An. 1875* (Dublin, 1877).

[32] *Census of Ireland, 1871* (Dublin, 1875).

[33] May 21, Aug. 22, 1850, Kirby Papers.

[34] Oct. 9, Dec. 8, 1852, Ibid.

[35] Dec. 20, 1852, Ibid.

[36] Jan. 28, 1853, Ibid.

[37] Mar. 17, 1853, Ibid.

[38] [June 1853], Ibid.

[39] Francis O'Neill to Kirby, Plymouth, July 13, 1853, Ibid. O'Neill was a native of Waterford, but when he was ordained after his studies in the Irish College in Rome he had to go on the English mission, because there was no place available for him in the diocese of Waterford. Though the following passage is both interesting and illustrative in many ways, the important point is that the Irish speakers in Plymouth wanted to remain psychologically whole in revealing the secrets of their hearts. "Please God I hope to have a place in Waterford next year; as one can effect more where there are good hearts. Here the English Catholics never look at an Irish priest, but we have the poor Paddies who are the support of this mission and without whom the Bishop, would have to leave this place. The Irish here are about three or four hundred. Some of them cannot be got to make their confessions in English, at this the Bishop is most indignant. He says that it is pride, and also because they make more of the priest than the Sacrament. He has to keep a priest who can speak Irish. I cannot put two words of it together so in that point I am no help. Were I sure of having this good Bishop always I would not think of returning to Ireland but as this is not at all likely especially as he is an old man I shall get my Exeat. He finds many faults with the Irish but they are the ones that we cannot deny. He speaks frequently about the way the priests in Ireland *demand* money for the Sacraments. This is no false charge against them for all whoever had any experience of the system even in our own Diocese and also of it even since the Thurles Synod will acknowledge that too much cannot be said against it."

[40] Thomas H. Burke, O.P., "The Supernatural Life of the Irish People," in *Lectures on Faith and Fatherland* (London, n.d.), 117. Father Burke lectured extensively in the United States in 1872.

[41] Sean O'Faolain, *King of the Beggars* (London, 1938), 367–68. In summing up the significance of O'Connell, O'Faolain wrote, "In whatever way one might try to define the ideal life of the Irish people, his image is likely to rise before the mind— always remembering that he came at the beginning and was only following his instinct in a groping use of the material to his hand. Lecky said that he studied men, not books; in studying men he found himself, and in finding himself he presented to his people a mirror of their reality. He is interesting in a hundred ways, but in no way more interesting than in this—that he was the greatest of all Irish realists who knew that if he could but once define, he would thereby create. He did define, and he did create. He thought a democracy and it rose. He defined himself, and his people became him. He imagined a future and the road appeared. He left his successors nothing to do but to follow him. They have added precision to his definition, but his definition is not altered; they have added to his methods, but his methods remain. You may break gold but it is gold still, fashion wood but it is wood still. The content of Irish life is the content of the Irish character, the dregs and the lees and the pure wine of this one man's recipe—to be purified indeed, to grow more rich in the wood with time, but never to lose the flavour of his reality, the composition of his mind."

[42] The author is at present engaged in writing a *History of the Roman Catholic Church in Ireland in the Nineteenth Century, 1780–1918*, in which he hopes to deal *in extenso* with this crucial relationship between nationalism and Catholicism as well as with many of the other themes only touched upon in this article.

[43] "The truth is, the Gaelic people of that century were not a mob, as every picture given of them, whether by historian or novelist, would lead one to think. They were mob-like in externals; and one forgives the historians if those externals threw them out, but how forgive the novelists? If not a mob what then were they? They were the residuary legatees of a civilisation that was more than a thousand years old. And this they knew; it was indeed the very pivot of all they did know, and the insult that followed on their poverty wounded them not only as human beings but as 'Children of Kings, Sons of Milesius!' ('Clanna righthe maca Mileadh'). With that civilisation

they were still in living contact, acquainted with its history; and such of its forms as had not become quite impossible in their way of life, they still piously practised, gradually changing the old moulds into new shapes, and, whether new or old, filling them with a content that was all of the passing day and their own fields. What of art they did create in their cabins is poor and meagre if compared with what their fathers had created in the Duns of Kings and Grianans of Queens; yet the hem matches the garment and the clasp the book. Here hinted, then, what these historians scanted; and scanting the soul and the spirit of a people, what of that people have they profitably to speak? But history has belied the historians, for that people, if they were but a mob, had died, and their nationality died with them: instead of which that nationality is vigorous today, not only at home, but in many lands abroad— 'translated, passed from the grave.'" Daniel Corkery, *The Hidden Ireland: A Study of Gaelic Munster in the Eighteen Century* (Dublin, 1925), 28–29.

[44] *Census of Ireland, 1861* (Dublin, 1863); *Census of Ireland, 1901* (Dublin, 1903).

[45] "Ireland has not only done a great deal during the past century for the Propagation of the Faith so that her missionaries and nuns and faithful people are now to be found foremost in everything good going on in the various missions of the old and new world but at present the whole country may be regarded as a vast recruiting field for sustaining these distant missions. We have in Kilkenny at present (to mention one instance) an American Christian Brother seeking for young men to join that order in the United States. They have at present *500* Irishmen among the Xtian Brothers of the United States and only 200 of all other nationalities. They have seven Colleges in the United States and the Superiors of them all are Irish. Nevertheless they are called the 'French Xtian Brothers.' At present they desire at least 50 more Irish postulants, as they find that none labour so zealously and efficiently in the American schools, as the Irish Brothers. The Brother has been only a few days in Ireland still he has already got twenty postulants. We have also a Nun of the Holy Cross who is seeking postulants in like manner. She told me that when she was over here two years ago she succeeded in getting *twenty-five* young ladies for her order in the United States, and that they all persevered. She now desires 25 more and has come over to search for them." Patrick Francis Moran to Kirby, Apr. 28, 1876, Kirby Papers.

[46] Donald H. Akenson, *The Irish Education Experiment: The National System of Education in the Nineteenth Century* (London, 1970), 140, 346. There are no average daily attendance figures before 1852. In 1852 the number of children on the rolls was 544,604, and average daily attendance was 282,575; the number of children on the rolls in 1840 had been 232,560. I have, therefore, assuming there was improvement, calculated average daily attendance at something less than half of 232,560.

[47] *Ibid.*, 377. These percentages, of course, are for that portion of the population over five years of age. See also William D. P. Bliss, ed., *The New Encyclopedia of Social Reform* (New York, 1908), 598. "The total illiteracy of immigrants [to the United States] over fourteen years of age, in 1905, was 26.2 per cent. The females are, in general, more illiterate than the males." The study then cites figures for "the illiteracy of the races contributing more than 2,000 immigrants . . . for the same year." The statistics, presented under the heading "Northern and Western Europe (Chiefly Teutonic and Celtic)," are as follows: Scandinavian 0.6; Scotch 0.7; English 1.3; Bohemian and Moravian 1.7; Finnish 1.8; French 2.7; Irish 3.8; German 4.2; Dutch and Flemish 5.3; Italian (North) 14.0; Average 3.7.

III

Church, State, and Nation
in Modern Ireland

In the two previous chapters I examined the economic and social power and influence of the Roman Catholic Church in Ireland in the nineteenth century.[1] The economic power and influence of the Church in Ireland proved to be formidable. Indeed, the Church had become stronger and stronger during the nineteenth century by building an imposing establishment in terms of both plant and personnel. All this was done, moreover, in a country that had not experienced an industrial revolution, had exported some five million people, and still remained in 1914 one of the more economically backward areas in Western Europe. On the social side the achievement of the Church in Ireland was perhaps even more impressive. In the course of the century the Church had managed to build itself into the very vitals of the nation by becoming almost at one with its identity. By 1914 Irish and Catholic had not only become interchangeable terms, but Catholic had come to be the inclusive term. The instrument for this great social change was a devotional revolution that made practicing Catholics of the Irish people in a generation and that eventually made Irish Catholicism a worldwide phenomenon in the English-speaking world.

In this chapter I will attempt to complete the historical trilogy by examining the nature and extent of the political power and influence of the Church in modern Ireland. The main difficulty in such an effort, however, is that for the history of modern Ireland there is as yet no satisfactory political frame within which the role of the Church can be examined. That such a frame has not yet been structured may seem at first surprising, especially since the political materials, unlike the economic and social, have apparently been both abundant and available for some time. On reflection, however, it becomes obvious that the reason why this has not been done is that without considering the Church, which in Ireland is integral to any such frame, it was impossible. In a word, the Church does not exist independently of the Irish political system, but it is one of the basic elements in that system. But what then are the other elements, besides the Church, that are necessary to the building of a satisfactory political frame, which will allow for a meaningful discussion of the nature and extent of the political power and influence of the Church in Ireland?

The other elements are essentially two—the nation and the state. In sustaining and shaping the identity of the first, and in helping to make and consolidate the power of the second, the Church has played a most vital part. Before proceeding, however, to the dynamic nature of the relationship between Church, state, and nation, some effort must be made to define the participants. Since the nation is at once the most allusive and inclusive term of the three, perhaps it would be best to begin with it. In order to escape the dilemma of defining the nation so broadly as to make the term virtually meaningless, I propose to define it here as that class of Irish Roman Catholic tenant farmers who since 1750 have occupied more than thirty acres. They are, in effect, the critical nation-forming class. The most remarkable thing about this class is not so much its size, but the apparent consistency with which it has maintained its numbers over the last two hundred years.[2] There are, of course, no reliable figures before 1845, but a glance at the table will make the position tolerably clear for at least the period since then. These figures must, of course, be qualified in that all those holding more than thirty acres were not Roman Catholics and the number of holdings was always greater than the number of occupiers of those holdings. Still, when all the estimates and deductions are made, this critical class has numbered something more than one hundred thousand, and if taken with its dependents, it has probably numbered about five hundred thousand over the last two hundred years.[3]

But what about the validity of projecting these figures backward in time from 1845 to 1750, especially when it is admitted that there are no reliable statistics before 1845? It is most fortunate that there are figures available for 1845 and 1847 because without them there would be no way of knowing what actual impact the Great Famine had on the Irish system of landholding. What is now obvious is that the famine did not much alter the position of those who held more than thirty acres, while it decimated those who held less, and especially those who held less than fifteen acres. But if the famine had little effect on the plus-thirty-acre tenant class as a class, were there not perhaps longer-term socioeconomic phenomena between 1750 and 1850 that had either a qualitative or quantitative impact? Did not population growth or price movements in response to market conditions, for example, have an effect? In terms of reducing the numbers of this critical class the answer would appear to be no.

The consensus among Irish economic historians is that the real economic watershed in modern Ireland was 1815 rather than 1847.[4] The fall in prices and the general depression between 1815 and 1820 precipitated a long-term trend away from tillage in favor of pasture. In the long run (that is, between 1815 and 1960) this trend certainly strengthened and even increased the number of farmers holding more than thirty acres, but the increase was probably marginal before the famine because of the continued increase in population and the consequent land hunger. But what effect did the substantial increase in prices, especially in corn, have on their numbers between 1780 and 1815? The shift from pasture to tillage in the face of favorable corn prices certainly drove rents up, but this did not mean that the larger farmers were under inordinate pressure, unless they could not find labor in sufficient quantity to enable them to convert to tillage. Since the increase in population provided a more than adequate supply of labor, there is good reason to suppose that the larger farmers prospered, especially if they held long-term leases that protected them against the substantial increase in rents.[5]

This is not to say, however, that the more than thirty acre tenant farmer class did not have an anxious time of it, especially after 1815. The fall in prices made it imperative for them to convert to pasture, and the continuing high rents made it difficult for them to find the capital to stock their farms. Still, given the increase in livestock figures between 1815 and 1850, it appears that these farmers responded well to the economic challenge.[6] Their ultimate anxiety, however, could only have been rooted in the incredible social conditions that developed after 1815. An ever-increasing and expanding culture of poverty, in the making since 1780, but masked

BREAKDOWN OF THE NUMBERS OF LANDHOLDERS OF MORE THAN ONE ACRE IN IRELAND, 1847–1960[a]

	1847	1861	1881	1901	1917	1941	1960
More than 1 and less than 5 acres	139,041	85,469	67,071	62,655	47,619	40,757	29,222
More than 5 and less than 15 acres	269,534	183,931	164,645	154,418	125,828	88,265	63,746
More than 15 and less than 30 acres	164,337	141,251	135,793	134,091	123,129	106,203	92,415
More than 30 acres	157,097	157,833	159,834	164,569	163,221	179,748	175,845
Total	730,009	568,484	527,343	515,733	459,797	414,973	361,228

[a] Sources for table: 1847, Agricultural Returns for Ireland, 1847, House of Commons (hereafter HC) (1847), 57: 111; 1861, Agricultural Statistics for Ireland, 1861, HC (1863), 69: 556, 1881, Agricultural Statistics for Ireland, 1881, HC (1882), 74: 93; 1901, Agricultural Statistics for Ireland, 1901, HC (1902), 116: pt. 1, p. 358; 1917, Agricultural Statistics for Ireland, 1917, HC (1921), 41: 14; 1941, 26 counties: Ireland (Eire), Department of Industry and Commerce, Statistical Abstract, 1942 (Dublin, 1942), 57; 6 counties: Great Britain, Ministry of Agriculture and Fisheries, Department of Agriculture for Scotland, Ministry of Agriculture, Northern Ireland, Agricultural Statistics, 1945: United Kingdom (London, 1948), pt. i, p. 29; 1960, 26 counties: Ireland (Eire), Central Statistics Office, Statistical Abstract of Ireland, 1964 (Dublin, 1964), 94; 6 counties: Ministry of Agriculture, Agricultural Statistics, quoted

in Ireland (Eire), Central Statistics Office, *Statistical Abstract of Ireland, 1964* (Dublin, 1864), app., p. 359. The very complex question of how homogeneous this tenant farmer class with more than 30 acres really was has not been taken up here because the primitive state of the evidence requires more research and thought and the scope of the question would demand yet another article. Even a cursory breakdown, however, of the 157,833 holdings of more than 30 acres in 1861, which may be taken in general as a representative year for the whole period since 1847, certainly reveals that there was an economic and social spectrum, though the meaning of that spectrum is not entirely clear. There were 72,449 tenant farmers with more than 30 and less than 50 acres; 53,933 with more than 50 and less than 100; 21,531 with more than 100 and less than 200; 8,329 with more than 200 and less than 500; and 1,591 with more than 500 acres. Whatever these figures may be forced to yield on analysis as to how homogeneous this class actually was, it is clear that equating the 500-acre farmer with the man who held between 30 and 50 acres is to take too simple a view. Still, when these figures are considered in the light of an expanding electorate in the counties between 1832 and 1885, on the basis of reducing property qualifications, it becomes obvious that the political center of gravity was located in this class, though in each succeeding political generation that center of gravity was located lower in the socioeconomic pyramid formed by this class. For example, the county electorate, which before the Reform Bill of 1832 numbered only about 20,000, was enlarged in that year to some 60,000, while in 1850 it was enlarged again to about 135,000. In 1868 this county electorate had expanded again to some 177,000 until it was finally democratized in 1884, when some 630,000 were enfranchised. Before 1850, therefore, Daniel O'Connell found his political center of gravity located largely in the 100-acre farmer, while Charles Stewart Parnell in the next political generation found his center of gravity in the 50-acre man; in our own day Eamon de Valera has found his in the 30-acre man. What makes this correlation even more significant, of course, is that the total Catholic population has shrunk from about 6,500,000 in O'Connell's day to something more than 3,000,000 in de Valera's day, and the more than 30-acre farmers, whose numbers have been more than maintained in the same period, have made up an increasingly larger proportion of the political whole.

by the prosperity before 1815, was then given another dimension by the fear of the smaller and more marginal farmer and especially his sons, who did not want to sink into a landless class and who desperately gave a lead to the resistance, which took the form of agrarian outrages and secret societies, against the tithes, high rents, and the conversion to pasture.[7] These fearful social conditions were given painful emphasis, moreover, by the periodic famines and harvest failures between 1815 and 1850. The quality, therefore, that distinguished the Irish Roman Catholic tenant farmers holding more than thirty acres both before the famine and since has been their endurance. In the face of all adversity, however, they have not only remained economically viable and maintained their numbers, but they have also emerged as the dominant political class in modern Ireland.

This nation-forming class, in fact, is the class for whom and by whom the Irish state, that second element necessary to the structuring of a satisfactory political frame for modern Irish history, was eventually created and consolidated. As a class they were first mobilized for political action in the 1820s by Daniel O'Connell in his Catholic Association.[8] What O'Connell understood, however, was that although this class was necessary, it was not, in the political context of his day, sufficient to the achievement of Emancipation. He therefore included the Roman Catholic clergy and involved the masses. By incorporating the clergy he secured the only institutional apparatus that permeated, however imperfectly, to the grass roots, and from the masses he acquired all the strength and menace implicit in their aggregate numbers. He won Emancipation in 1829, therefore, because he was able to assemble in his Catholic Association a unified national political phalanx whose purpose was sanctioned by a very considerable and influential body of British public opinion in and out of Parliament. When O'Connell, however, attempted to apply the same formula in launching the agitation for the repeal of the Act of Union on the heels of winning Emancipation, he was unsuccessful. He was never able, in fact, to mobilize his national political phalanx again, and when he appeared to have done so in 1843, the leviathan proved to have only feet of clay.[9]

Why O'Connell was never able, beyond appearances, to create a repeal movement equal to the one for Emancipation is one of the critical questions in modern Irish history because the answer to it not only explains his failure, but the eventual success of those who later assumed his mantle as leader. Two reasons are central in explaining O'Connell's failure: first, he never received from the clergy, and especially the bishops, that complete commitment on repeal which he had secured for Emancipation; second, he never won the support of any considerable or influential body of British public opinion for repeal as had existed for Emancipation. From the moment O'Connell launched his repeal agitation in late 1829 and throughout the decade of the 1830s, the bishops as a body were extremely cautious about any further political involvement.[10] Early in 1834, when O'Connell had been agitating repeal for over four years, the bishops formally capped their caution at their annual meeting by forbidding the use of Catholic chapels for political purposes and exhorting their priests to abstain from those political activities that were not in keeping with their calling.[11] O'Connell's inability either to persuade or to coerce the bishops as a body into supporting repeal was undoubtedly a major consideration in his decision early in 1835 to drop repeal and "test the Union" by giving the new Whig government under Lord Melbourne an opportunity to redress Irish grievances.

When O'Connell once again renewed agitation for repeal early in 1840, he secured the support and public approbation of the influential archbishop of Tuam, John MacHale. In time he also received, in a hierarchy of twenty-seven, the adherence of some fifteen other bishops.[12] Despite the apparent increase in both unity and power that the adhesion of a majority of the bishops brought to the repeal movement, the alliance proved costly to O'Connell because Archbishop MacHale was as much interested, and perhaps more successful, in using O'Connell for his religious purposes than O'Connell was in using the archbishop for his political purposes. Not only did the religious exclusiveness of MacHale eventually alienate the liberal Protestant and Young Ireland components of the Repeal Association, but the large and influential minority among the bishops, disliking and perhaps even fearing the archbishop of Tuam's attempt to impose his religious and political views on them, never acquiesced in the alliance and never became members of the Repeal Association. When Rome in late 1844 finally condemned the overaggressive political activities of the majority among the Irish bishops and priests and Sir Robert Peel, meanwhile, introduced a series of measures designed to satisfy the needs of the more politically conservative among the Irish bishops, the divisions in the hierarchy were not only deepened, but the already imperfect clerical component of the Repeal Association was further impaired.[13]

While O'Connell was thus having great difficulty mobilizing and sustaining his national political phalanx between 1829 and 1844, he had even less success in converting any considerable or influential body of public opinion in Britain to the cause of repeal.[14] His response to the challenge of converting British public opinion was the creation of an Irish party in the House of Commons. Though numbering between thirty and forty in the decade of the 1830s and a mainstay of the Whig government after 1835, the party's impact was slight in educating British public opinion to the virtues of repeal before it was decimated in the general election of 1841. The reason why a large part of British public opinion reacted differently to Emancipation than it had to repeal was that the former was about liberty and freedom while the latter was essentially a question of sovereignty. This is why both Whigs and Radicals could consistently structure political alliances with O'Connell whenever he eschewed repeal and advocated reform. The potential danger, however, in all such extraparliamentary associations ran deep with those British politicians and statesmen who still thought partially in terms of the eighteenth-century constitution and who remembered the American and Irish debacles of another generation.[15] Whether they were called associations, societies, congresses, or conventions, there was a tendency in them to usurp the legitimate authority of Parliament. O'Connell's Catholic Association was no exception, and it was legally harassed before the passage of Emancipation and duly suppressed when Emancipation became law.

If the Catholic Association aroused the worst fears of responsible British politicians, the Repeal Association confirmed them. O'Connell was not only attempting to set the law at defiance, but he was now trying to impose it on Parliament by invoking as his sanction that most dangerous principle, the legitimacy of "opinion out of doors" become popular sovereignty. Moreover, when he and his association took upon themselves the responsibility of maintaining order in Ireland as well as sanctioning law, they were in a fair position to claim to be the *de facto* power. In such a situation all that remained necessary for the creation of an embryo state was the effective crystallization of the local and national political apparatus in the will of the "leader," who would then emerge as the *de facto* head of state. The important point to be made here, however, is that without the support of a significant body of politically responsible public opinion in Britain, no Irish issue—whether about civil liberty or where ultimate power lay—was constitutionally viable. In other words, to confront a British government by creating a *de facto* control, or an embryo state, in Ireland was simply not enough because a constitutional settlement of any Irish question was ultimately dependent on a *de jure* ratification by a majority in the imperial Parliament.

O'Connell's real significance does not lie in what he was unable to achieve, but rather in the various means he devised to accomplish his ends. The means, products of an incredibly fertile political imagination, were his real legacy to his political posterity. He made participatory democracy as real in Ireland as he made the Irish party viable in the House of Commons. Moreover, in 1828 and 1829 he created a stable embryo Irish state, and he very nearly did it again in 1843. On both occasions he was undisputed leader of his people, he taxed them, and, through his assumption of quasi-judicial and quasi-police functions, he made himself and his political apparatus responsible for law and order.[16] With Emancipation his embryo state simply dissolved because the end for which it had been organized was achieved. His attempt to put together for repeal that same combination of large and small tenant farmers, high and low clergy, city merchants and country shopkeepers, liberal Protestants and ecumenical Catholics, and the men of no property, that large, though less-respectable class, was frustrated because important segments of this combination did not really believe in repeal as a practical end, especially if the alternative was civil war.[17] Still, O'Connell could find some solace in the fact that the combination of the larger tenant farmers and the lower clergy had generally proven steadfast in its support of repeal. His fundamental political strength, in truth, was always found in the south and west where this combination was most formidable, and in effecting this combination he provided the real basis for any nationalist movement in the future.[18] In this, then, as in so much else, O'Connell showed his successors the way in which an Irish state might be made without actually resorting to insurrection. His ultimate tragedy was that in the face of incredibly adverse circumstances he could neither mobilize his materials nor synchronize his means to bring about this end.

The lessons taught by Daniel O'Connell in his efforts to create an Irish state seemed to have been lost on the political generation that succeeded him, but the appearance belied the reality. Actually, the third quarter of the nineteenth century in Ireland was the period between seedtime and harvest. Those elements of weakness that had so hampered O'Connell were either corrected or eliminated, and Irish society between 1850 and 1875, at least on the Catholic and nationalist side, became both more prosperous and homogeneous. The culture of poverty that had been in the making since 1780 was virtually liquidated after 1850 through emigration, and the marginal tenant farmers were forced to the same extreme through eviction. The larger tenant farmers were not only thus enabled to consolidate their holdings, but they were freer to convert from tillage to pasture and thereby reap the profits available in the strong and steady prices sustained by the demand of the British market for their products. The great reduction in the number of laborers, cottiers, and marginal farmers after 1850 also resulted in Irish society becoming more homogeneous as well as prosperous. The breaking up of the culture of poverty at the famine, for example, not only resulted in Irish society as a whole becoming more respectable or "lace curtain," but Gaelic Ireland also received a blow in that social catastrophe from which it never recovered. The larger tenant farmers, therefore, not only became the dominant political and economic class after 1850, but they became the dominant social and cultural class as well.

The Church, the third element necessary to the structuring of a satisfactory political frame, was crucial in helping to effect this social and cultural homogeneity of the nation. But when one speaks of the Irish Church, what does one actually mean? What is meant here are the people in the Church who counted, and those who counted were the active as distinguished from the passive—the bishops, the priests, and the larger tenant farmers, or the nation-forming class. They counted, moreover, in that order. At the base of the pyramid were the larger tenant farmers, who not only provided the Church with its main financial support and staffed it with their sons and daughters, but who were always its practicing and devotional nucleus.[19] In the late eighteenth century this class, allied with its cousinhood in the towns, probably numbered about seven hundred thousand in a Catholic population of three million. By 1845 they still numbered less than a million in a Catholic population that had increased to nearly seven million. Each decade after the famine, however, their numerical situation improved absolutely and relatively. In 1850, for example, they numbered nearly one million in five, while by 1900 they numbered about one million in three of the Catholic population. In the light of this improving numerical relationship it is easier, therefore, to understand how the Church between 1850 and 1875 was able to effect a devotional revolution that made practicing Catholics of Irish men, women, and children and to become in the process psychologically almost at one with the nation's identity as Irish and Catholic became virtually synonymous. But if the larger tenant farmers provided the sinews of the Church, it can hardly be said that they spoke for it. Even at the risk of some obvious distortion, however, it may be fairly asserted that at least the voice of the Church, if not its mind, was increasingly found in the *coetus episcoporum*, or the bishops as a body. This assertion is justified to some extent by the fact that one of the most significant themes in the history of the Irish Church in the nineteenth century was the increase in episcopal authority, especially vis-à-vis the priests. Moreover, given the mode of nomination by the senior clergy of a diocese and the report by the bishops of the province for the authoritative decision of Rome, the Irish bishops as a body were generally representative of the clergy. Finally, when the Irish bishops spoke as a body they were always understood to be speaking authoritatively for the Irish Church. With this modified, though traditional *clerico e laico*, working definition of the Irish Church in hand, it is now possible to attempt to explain how indeed the Church itself became unified in the process of making practicing Catholics of the Irish people in a generation.

Two factors were crucial in this process. The first was the founding of the national seminary at Maynooth in 1795; the second was the appointment in late 1849 of Paul Cullen as archbishop of Armagh and apostolic delegate to the Holy See. The former resulted in the Irish Church acquiring over the years a more uniform and better-disciplined priesthood, while the latter finally effected that authoritative control in the Irish Church that was being striven for in the universal Church at the same time by Pius IX. Between 1795 and 1845 Maynooth provided the Irish Church with perhaps something more than half the priests it needed. After 1845, as a result of Sir Robert Peel's increased grant, Maynooth produced priests enough, in the face of a declining population, to provide for the whole of the Irish Church. By 1850, for example, the great majority of the bishops, and by 1875 the great majority of the priests, on the Irish mission had been trained at Maynooth.[20] But what was even more important than the impressive increase in numbers was that Maynooth came to produce the Irish priest and the values that corresponded to that prototype.

But what indeed were the values of the Maynooth priest? He was at once a patriot in politics and a rigorist in his moral theology. "There are two things," Aiden Devereaux, an Irish priest trained in Rome, wrote Paul Cullen, rector of the Irish College there on September 19, 1836, "which the Roman students on their return to this mission will help to do. Namely to put down a spirit of disregard to Papal authority which during the last twenty years is beginning to spring up in the minds of some of the younger and more ignorant of the clergy and a spirit of rigorism which has been introduced into the national seminaries by French Professors and their disciples."

> Amongst a Conference composed of such persons as these if a Roman student maintains for instance that ". . . the *precept* of the Church is fulfilled by hearing Mass on a Sunday" and that "anything further although most earnestly to be recommended as a matter of counsel is not to be enjoined under pain of Mortal sin in the tribunal" he would be looked upon as next door to impiety and yet I have heard the professors and preachers in Rome preach and teach that proposition most emphatically. The Roman opinion however cannot fail to operate as a check upon extremes of either class and amongst the more rational and unprejudiced cannot fail to have due weight.[21]

The rigorism Father Devereaux complained about has been aptly described as "the moral system of those who draw too tightly the reins of law in restriction of a man's natural liberty of action; who are inclined to make precepts out of counsels, and mortal sins out of venial ones. In cases of doubt, whether as to the law or the fact they hold that the law is binding until the doubt is cleared up in favour of liberty; and thus they impose an intolerable burden on men, especially on scrupulous and conscientious men, whose doubts are often imaginary, and if yielded to may go far to destroy the peace of their conscience and the happiness of their lives."[22] There is little doubt that there was a tendency toward rigorism in the early moral teaching at Maynooth. That the success of such teaching there, however, can be attributed entirely to the French-trained professors and their textbooks is doubtful. The rigorism that pervaded the teaching at Maynooth was also the result of the growing awareness on the part of the bishops of the need to meet the requirements of the Irish mission. The geometrical increase in the population after 1800 obviously required more priests, but given the arithmetical nature of the supply, they must also be better disciplined and more attentive in their pastoral duties. Given the launching in 1820, moreover, of the New Reformation in Ireland by the Protestant evangelicals or "Biblicals," a more learned and articulate clergy was also required. Maynooth responded to the challenge, and the result of providing a better-educated, disciplined, and pastorally attentive clergy was to produce a more morally rigorous one as well. In brief, the French-trained professors at Maynooth were as much involved in meeting a real pastoral need as in providing a stricter system of moral theology.

The brand of patriotism, however, that developed at Maynooth after 1815 had a more positive side to it than merely a Gallic disregard for the authority of the pope as described by Father Devereaux. The struggle against the veto, the launching of the New Reformation by the Protestant evangelicals, and the campaign for Catholic Emancipation successively deepened the national consciousness of the Irish clergy in general and the faculty and students at Maynooth in particular.[23] When O'Connell launched his agitation for repeal in late 1829, however, the older generation of priests, who had been trained on the Continent, drew back and attempted to distinguish between what was politico-religious and purely political. Given the fact, moreover, that the Irish bishops then closed their chapels to repeal agitation and exhorted their clergy to restrain themselves with regard to it, and also that Maynooth was a government-subsidized institution, the faculty and students there naturally assumed a low profile in politics in deference to both ecclesiastical and governmental authority. The nationalist leaven continued to work, however, for by 1843 the faculty were apparently nearly all moderate Repealers, and if Thomas Cullen, a young seminarian, was a fair example, the students were even more ardent. "There is no talk," Thomas enthusiastically assured his first cousin, Paul Cullen in Rome, from Maynooth on May 20, 1843, "about anything else but Dan and Repeal."[24] "Dr. Higgins," he reported, referring to the bishop of Ardagh and Clonmacnoise, "made a most violent speech on Sunday last before a *100 000* men in which he stated that all the bishops of Ireland were out and out repealers." "It is the common opinion in Ireland," Thomas then added, "that we will either have the union repealed or a civil war before the close of this year."

All the tory Journals are preaching up the doctrine of *assassination* as the only means of saving Ireland from a civil war. They say Dan should be sacrificed on the altar of repeal. I hope you will recommend him to the prayers of every well wisher of his native land, poor Ireland. He is doing wonders for the regeneration of this country and if the

Almighty in his mercy spares him for a few years longer I have no doubt but that we will live to see Ireland what nature destined her to be "An nation/great, glorious and free/first flower of the/earth and first gem/of the sea."

"The bishop," Thomas concluded, referring to their common diocesan, Francis Haly, the bishop of Kildare and Leighlin, "is as yet a non repealer and of course is keeping back the clergy of our diocese."[25]

The faculty of Maynooth were naturally somewhat more prudent in their advocacy of repeal. For example, Charles W. Russell, professor of humanity at Maynooth and later its president for twenty-three years, arrived home at the climax of O'Connell's agitation in the late summer of 1843 after an extended stay in Rome on personal business. "My journey homewards," he reported on August 28 to Paul Cullen, his host in Rome, "& what I have seen since & heard, have made me a confirmed repealer." "It is far harder," he explained to Cullen, "to *see ahead* here than it was in Rome: but everyone agrees that *something must come of it*. I am inclined to think it must come *itself*; though I cannot even guess how."[26] Less than a month later Russell wrote Cullen again explaining that though repeal was far stronger than when he last wrote, he thought that "even still, *instalments* will be gladly taken." "The meetings are as *monstrous* as ever," he noted further, "& what I look upon as the strongest sign of the times, the non-repealers are growing louder & louder in their calls for *justice*. This class is now very generally falling into the *federalist* party." "We are here," he assured Cullen in conclusion, distinguishing between his own party and the radical Repealers, or Young Irelanders, "with hardly an exception moderate men."[27] In the last analysis, then, what was created at Maynooth was a commitment to constitutional nationalism that precluded the physical-force tradition in modern Irish politics.

While the Irish Church was thus being unified by Maynooth from the bottom up in terms of its personnel and its values, Pius IX, in terms of authority, proceeded to complement that development from the top down by appointing Paul Cullen archbishop of Armagh and apostolic delegate in late 1849. With the accession of Cullen the quarrels that had resulted in a civil war among the bishops in the Irish Church in the 1840s began to subside, and by the time he died a cardinal in late 1878 Cullen had succeeded in creating an episcopal body from which to dissent in public or in the press, on the part of either a bishop or a priest, would have constituted a grave ecclesiastical scandal. The critical subject, of course, on which the Irish Church, under the leadership of Cullen and through the bishops as a body, learned to speak with one voice and one mind was the education question. Between 1850 and 1878 Cullen, who had been translated to Dublin in 1852, devoted a large part of his energies to modifying, if he could not eliminate, state control over education. When, for example, the bishop of Kerry, David Moriarty, who was not at one with Cullen on the education question, wrote him complaining that it was not wise to discourage Catholics from serving as commissioners on the National Board of Education, Cullen firmly pointed out what he thought was the correct policy. "In reply," he informed Moriarty from Dublin on October 7, 1860, "I beg to assure you that I have not used my influence to prevent good Catholics from joining the board. I leave them altogether to their own discretion." "However," Cullen noted, "I see a great objection to accepting office, which I cannot remove." "Those who become commissioners," he explained, "are I suppose, pledged to maintain the system as it is. They must uphold the model schools, and in doing so they throw the formation of all masters into the hands of a protestant government, and they contribute as far as in them lies, to undermine Catholicity in the country."

> Your Lordship says that all gentry of the country are against the Bishops. Fortunately the gentry do not represent the country—they are few, and I believe they were as much for the Veto as they are for mixed or infidel education.
>
> Your Lordship is afraid that the Irish Cavour Party may get hold of the system. I entertain the same fear, and I think we ought all to fear such a result as long as we are at the mercy of a Palmerston or any other English minister. Such ministers may appoint Cavourites any day they wish according to the present system.
>
> As the system is working actually it is in Protestant and Presbyterian hands, and the Catholics who were on the board and who were quite as zealous as those now spoken of, did not, perhaps could not, prevent the system from being made much more dangerous than it was in the beginning.
>
> Hopes of changes are now held out but if they are really intended, why are they not officially announced.

"As long," Cullen finally declared, "as the model schools and training schools are maintained, I will oppose the system." "I trust," he warned, "to be able very soon to assail openly the model schools in this city. I will do it by ecclesiastical censures as soon as matters will be ripe for such a step."[28]

Why Cullen was able to have his way in the long run, however, was that he was just as prudent as he was patient and determined. When, for example, his faithful friend and successor as rector of the Irish College in Rome, Tobias Kirby, wrote him late in the summer of 1862 suggesting that the problem of infidel education would be soon solved if the clergy withdrew their schools from all connection with the government, Cullen immediately made it clear not only what the results of such rash action would be, but what indeed the consequences of such a course had been in the past. "You appear to think," he wrote Kirby, "that it wd be an easy matter to withdraw the children from all the National Schools." "It wd.," Cullen explained, "be almost impossible, and it wd be very dangerous to attempt it."

> Imprimis you cd not get either Bishops or priests to agree on such a step—posso if you refuse the grant, the schools wd be closed, as it wd be impossible to collect the amount. In some parishes there are 10 schools—which receive £30 or £40 each, that is £300 or £400 per an. and in the same parishes all the art of man wd not succeed in collecting £100 per an for schools such is the poverty of the people.
>
> As to the model schools, the country ones and the small ones can be put down readily. The big ones cannot be put down until there will be other schools to receive the children. They can be discredited and checked and when there will be other schools for the children, they may be prohibited but it is not safe to do anything unless where success is certain. Everything can be done gradually, but if we fail in any attempt, we lose immensely—If the Bishops who assailed the System in 1837 to 1845 had gone on cautiously and quietly, instead of recurring to violent denunciations they wd have done good service, whereas they failed in everything.

"Now thanks be to God," Cullen concluded, "all who were offended by past violence are coming round—and as we are becoming unanimous everything may be done by degrees."[29]

When the government, in fact, only five years later asked the bishop of Kerry whether he would consent to serve on a royal commission to inquire into and report on the national system of primary education, he prudently wrote Cullen asking for his advice. Cullen refused to be drawn into the question and adroitly suggested instead that Moriarty ask the opinion of the body of the bishops who were just about to meet. When the bishops advised against his accepting and Moriarty then deferred to his colleagues,[30] Russell, the president of Maynooth, also declined the government's invitation. Such was the ascendancy that Cullen, now a cardinal, had achieved by 1867 among the clergy on the education question. His total achievement was, in fact, quite impressive. In less than a generation he had not only insisted on building and maintaining, at enormous cost, a Catholic intermediate and university system in order to prevent the state from further encroaching in those areas, but he tenaciously resisted all efforts by the Board of National Education, which was responsible for the national system of primary education, to expand its control, while he attempted to do as much as he could to undermine its authority. He built, moreover, and again at enormous cost, a large diocesan seminary at Clonliffe because he disliked being too dependent for the training of his clergy on Maynooth, which up until 1869, at least, remained a state-subsidized institution. What Cullen was really opposed to, however, was not just state control over education, but any form of lay control over education, whether English or Irish.[31] Still, Cullen was able to have his way with regard to education for Catholics in Ireland because his policy was essentially a national one. He was in effect demanding Home Rule in a crucial social area, an area, moreover, that would be vital to the infrastructure of a *de facto* Irish state whenever it emerged. In any case, by the time the cardinal died in 1878, the education that existed for Catholics in Ireland was largely controlled by the Church.

The other subject on which the cardinal had equally strong convictions was the Irish Republican, or Fenian, brotherhood. He did not, however, manage to carry the Irish clergy so completely with him in the condemnation of Fenianism as he had on mixed education.[32] Several of the bishops, including the archbishop of Tuam, John MacHale, and a considerable number of the lower clergy were loath to condemn the Fenians because they were afraid such action would lessen their influence with their people. One of Cullen's most loyal supporters on the education question, William Keane, bishop of Cloyne, for example, had quietly ordered his priests in late 1865 not to denounce the Fenians.[33] In writing to Kirby in Rome shortly after, Keane cautiously attempted to explain how difficult the situation had become. "The first question of the day," he solemnly informed Kirby on February 6, 1866, from Queenstown, "is that of 'Fenianism.'" "It is destined," Keane prophesied, "to exercise an extraordinary influence on the future relations between priests and people." "The mass of the public," he explained to Kirby, "down to the very children going to school, are either Fenians or sympathise with the Fenians, not because they wish to give up the faith, or to neglect their religious duties, but because they hate England the enemy of their country and of their creed, and of the Holy Father and of everything Catholic, and because the Fenians are opposed to England." "If once the masses," Keane then warned in conclusion, "throw off the respect they always had for their priests, then will come the real Irish difficulty for England and for all concerned."[34]

The real significance of Fenianism, however, has been clouded by the quarrel of the Church with it. Fenianism was above all a class movement composed of laborers, cottiers, marginal farmers in the country, mechanics, tradesmen, and clerks in the towns, and enlisted men in the British army.[35] What the brotherhood achieved, in effect, was the politicization in the national interest of that still large but now more respectable class, the men of no property. In other words, it politicized what was left of a class that before the famine had tended to degenerate into the terrorism of agrarian secret societies. Clearing the countryside through eviction and emigration tended to locate the strength and influence of Fenianism in Irish towns and among the Irish proletariat in Britain and America, and this made Fenianism appear to be a more urban phenomenon than perhaps it really was. As an oath-bound secret society, of course, the brotherhood was condemned by the Church, but this was not what was really at the heart of their quarrel. Cardinal Cullen not only had a horror of lay control over education, but he also had a horror, strongly reinforced by his actual experience in Rome in 1849 with the republic of Mazzini, of a revolutionary lay ascendancy over the affections of the poor (read "ignorant"). In the mind of Cullen, the Fenians posed just such a threat.[36] The cardinal's very real concern for the poor was intermingled with a deeper concern for their obvious susceptibility to unprincipled agitators, who would use them for their own ends by playing on their patriotism and eventually, as had been and still was the case in the Papal States, threaten their faith by undermining the power and influence of the clergy. As the cardinal and the Irish clergy, therefore, attempted to deepen their devotional revolution and make Irish Catholicism less a class and more a national phenomenon, they competed with the Fenians for the affections of the same constituency. What has also been overlooked in this contest between Church and brotherhood, however, is that both were making a fundamental contribution to the creation of a homogeneous national consciousness that transcended class. The Church had indeed created an Irish Catholicism that included the men of no property, while the brotherhood guaranteed the commitment of the most able and articulate members of that class to the idea of an Irish state as a "Republic now virtually established." In other words, neither the Church nor the brotherhood, for their own reasons, allowed status or property to stand in the way of their conception of the national ideal.

What had been created then between 1850 and 1878 was a wealthier, better-educated, and more practically Catholic Irish national community that was as yet unable to focus on its political end—an Irish state. This inability to focus was a result of serious differences in the community over means, whether constitutional in terms of repeal or federalism or revolutionary in terms of a Fenian republic. Until some consensus emerged, therefore, the end remained only an idea. The circumstances which eventually produced that consensus, however, were not long in coming. The three successive harvest failures in Ireland between 1877 and 1879 along with the collapse of world agricultural prices because of competition from the New World radicalized both the laborers and the tenant farmers. The former were faced with the poor house and the latter with eviction, and both with emigration if they were to survive. The crisis resulted in the emergence of Charles Stewart Parnell as the leader of a combined agrarian and political movement. For several years Parnell had been attempting to provide the policy on which the Irish nation could focus and effect a political consensus.[37] He argued for the adoption of a middle course between the tame, submissive constitutionalism of Isaac Butt and the physical-force methods of the Fenians. He maintained that an active policy in the House of Commons, consisting of obstruction and intimidation, would not only bring the attention of the British government to Irish grievances, but it would soon make it realize that Irish business might be better done in Dublin than at Westminster, and certainly at less inconvenience to British legislation. What the British really respected, Parnell further argued, was power, and in the House of Commons power was found in numbers. Home Rule then would only come as a result of the creation of a disciplined Irish party in the House of Commons backed by the determined will of the Irish people organized in an irresistible national political phalanx.

In the seven short years between his taking up the combined leadership of the Land League and the Home Rule movements in

1879 and the introduction of Gladstone's first Home Rule Bill in 1886, Parnell created the modern Irish state. He was able to achieve what O'Connell had failed to do in the decades of the 1830s and 1840s not only because he was better favored by time and circumstance, but also because, like O'Connell, he was a politician of genius. For in the Land League of 1879 and 1880 he successfully focused a national political consciousness by creating a genuine national grass-roots organization that made every Catholic tenant farmer and shopkeeper realize that they not only had something to defend together as farmers and shopkeepers, but something to aspire to as Irishmen.[38] Between 1882 and 1885, furthermore, Parnell structured and contained that consciousness he had focused in the Land League by creating a national and local political apparatus that gave both substance and coherence to the idea of a *de facto* Irish state. Through the Irish National League, which he founded in 1882 after the suppression of the Land League and which rapidly established branches in nearly every parish in Ireland, Parnell eventually made himself and his party responsible for the administration of law and the maintenance of order. Through the league, for example, Parnell and his party administered Gladstone's Land Act of 1881, seized control of the great majority of Poor Law Guardian Boards outside of Protestant Ulster, and executed rough justice on those who would dare defy the league's law with respect to evictions and land-grabbing. By 1885, despite three years of renewed coercion acts on the part of Gladstone's Liberal government, law and order in Ireland depended more on Parnell and his party than it did on Her Majesty's viceroy and his Irish executive. When, indeed, the Conservative government, which succeeded after the fall of Gladstone's ministry in the summer of 1885, allowed the Coercion Act to lapse as the *quid pro quo* for Irish support in the House of Commons, actual *de facto* political control in Ireland fell to Parnell and his party.[39] Finally, in the general elections of 1885 and 1886, Parnell crystallized in his person as leader and institutionalized in the Irish Parliamentary party the deep conviction among Irishmen that their state would soon be as legal as it was then real.

The conversion of the Irish clergy in this great political revival was perhaps, after the containment of land agitation, the most significant factor in the creation of the Irish state.[40] Though the vast majority of the junior clergy, a smaller majority of the senior clergy, and minority of the bishops soon committed themselves to the Land League, a majority of the bishops, perhaps eighteen in a hierarchy of twenty-eight, remained either hostile or suspicious. The majority, moreover, were reinforced in their numbers by the knowledge that their attitude was approved of at Rome. Whatever their initial advantages, however, the majority soon found that their position was virtually untenable. If they refused to allow their priests to participate in the league, the initiative would be seized by socialists, Fenians, Protestants, and what was perhaps even worse, "Godless nobodies." John MacEvilly, bishop of Galway and coadjutor to the archbishop of Tuam, explained the dilemma the majority faced in a long letter to Kirby in Rome soon after the league was founded. "Whether the priests will it or no," MacEvilly reported on December 11, 1879, "the meetings will be held. Their people will assemble under the pressure of threatened famine to expound their wrongs to landlords and government; if the priests keep aloof these meetings will be scenes of disorder; if the priests attend they will keep the people attached to them." MacEvilly then went on to caution Kirby about any interference with the agitation on the part of Rome. "It would render the H. See," he warned, "very odious to seem to be influenced by the English against those who sacrificed everything for the Faith, and when the *general evictions* come, as come they will, in some districts, it would ruin us, if the [Roman] authorities could be quoted as against our people." "*Religion in this country*," he prophesied solemnly in conclusion, "*would never get over it.*"[41]

While the majority of the bishops, like MacEvilly, continued to refuse to have anything personally to do with the league, though they allowed their priests to participate, their position in the next three years was slowly eroded. Their confidence both in the British government and in Rome was undermined by the ineptness of the former in dealing with Irish discontent through coercion and the efforts of the latter to establish diplomatic relations with the British government against the unanimous and formal advice of the Irish bishops as a body. At the same time, Parnell was astutely courting the more conservative of the clergy by playing down his former role of agrarian agitator and building up his new image of a politician firmly committed to constitutional methods and devoted to denominational education.[42] By the summer of 1884, therefore, the bishops as a body were finally ready to come to terms with Parnell and his party. At their annual general meeting at Maynooth in October, besides the usual string of resolutions on the education question, the bishops also resolved "that we call upon the Irish parliamentary party to bring the above resolutions under the notice of the House of Commons, and to urge generally upon the government the hitherto unsatisfied claims of Catholic Ireland in all branches of the educational question."[43] Why the bishops resolved as they did was explained some weeks later by MacEvilly to Kirby. "Some parties," MacEvilly noted on October 26, "affect to be scandalized as the Irish Bishops at the Synod placing the Education question in the hands of the Irish Party. But the fact is, many of the Bishops, who, like myself, never joined the Irish Party, feel that there is no other possible way of gaining our rights from a government that will give Catholics nothing from love."[44]

The result of this move on the part of the bishops was the making of a very effective, if informal, clerical-nationalist alliance. The fact that the alliance was based on an understanding rather than on a formal agreement certainly obscures its terms though it does not make them any less real. As far as the bishops were concerned, they understood they had an explicit undertaking on the part of the party, that the initiative with regard to the education question on all its levels would rest with them. On the other hand, the party was implicitly assured in the bishops' formal request for its support on the education question that all doubts were now removed—about either the party's constitutional character or its aims with regard to achieving Home Rule and the settlement of the land question, and that, therefore, those bishops and priests who were inclined to commit themselves to the party and its program were completely free to do so. What Home Rule meant specifically or what might be a satisfactory settlement of the land question was, in fact, only worked out pragmatically in the next few years. By the fall of 1886, however, the bishops had defined their position both with regard to the party and its program. They had not only endorsed the party's lead on the question of Home Rule and approved the system of purchase as a final solution to the land question, but they had also established their individual right to be consulted as to the suitability of the parliamentary candidates selected by convention within their spiritual jurisdiction as well as spelling out specifically their clergy's role as clergy in the approval of those candidates in convention.

By 1886, then, the British state had lost the great game it had played for so many centuries in Ireland. An Irish state had not only been created in the minds of most Irishmen, but the national and local political apparatus necessary to the functioning of that state was operative. The apparatus, moreover, was entirely in the hands of Parnell and his party. When Gladstone proceeded to give those executive, legislative, and judicial functions form in the first Home Rule Bill, final notice was given that the ratification of the substance of that state by the British Parliament was really only a matter of time. After 1886, therefore, to talk about a solution to the Irish question, other than self-government, was not to face up to the realities of Irish political life. The crucial point to be made here, however, is that the Irish state could not have been made stable before 1886 if the Irish clergy had not been accommodated. If the Irish clergy, moreover, had not accepted the accommodation when it did, the character of the Irish state would have been a great deal different from what it eventually became.

In early accepting its place in the Irish state, the Church, for example, prevented that state from being eventually turned into the worst kind of autocracy by either the leader or the party. In the development of a concept of leader, a one-party system, a mass machine organization, a controlled press, and a single-plank national program, Ireland was certainly not unique among those nations struggling to become states in the modern world. In Ireland, however, because the revolution in the making of the state was constitutional rather than violent, the politics of dissent gave way to the politics of consensus rather than to the tyranny of the general will. What later saved the Irish state, both during and after the fall and death of Parnell, from the tyranny of either the leader, the party, or even the majority was that in the last analysis the bishops had enough real power and influence in the country to resist effectively any attempt by either the party or the leader to impose their will unilaterally on the others in the consensus. What really evolved, then, in the making of the Irish state was a unique constitutional balance that became basic to the functioning of the Irish political system.

But what of the needs of the nation in the aftermath of the making and the consolidating of the *de facto* Irish state by Parnell? By 1914 that nation-forming class, those Catholic tenant farmers holding more than thirty acres, were virtually all in the process of becoming owners of their holdings under the recent and various land purchase acts. Their new status, moreover, was reinforced and cushioned by the establishment at the same time of a buffer class of nearly three hundred thousand smaller farmers, holding between five and thirty acres, who were also becoming, however marginal and vulnerable, new property owners through the system of purchase.[45] The Church, furthermore, by 1914 had also achieved its heart's desire. With the establishment of the National University in 1908 the Church had finally achieved effective control on all levels of what was now really a system of denominational education financed by the state.[46] Indeed, the clerical-nationalist alliance had paid handsome dividends as far as the larger tenant farmers and the clergy were concerned.

Soon after the death of Parnell, however, and in the decade of the 1890s, there began to emerge in piecemeal fashion a growing number of small, diverse, and articulate groups who began to argue that the deeper needs of the nation were not being met by the dominant political consensus. In cumulative fashion they insisted, and more intensely after 1900, that the real task was nation building and that it could only be accomplished by the nation recovering its primeval identity, which was still rooted in what was left of its ancient Gaelic cultural heritage. What actually took place, then, was a revival of cultural nationalism generally described as the Irish-Ireland movement. In an incredible burst of national energy the Gaelic League, the Gaelic Athletic Association, the Irish Labour Movement, the Irish Agricultural Organizational Society, the Abbey Theatre, the All for Ireland League, Sinn Fein, the Independent Orange Order, the Ancient Order of Hibernians, the Socialist party of Ireland, and a host of others, all vied with each other in their efforts to make Ireland more conscious of its being Irish. Though the various groups represented a wide spectrum of the nation's interests, and often sneered at and quarreled with each other, they were all certainly one in espousing at least the need to revive the Irish language and to recover their lost cultural inheritance.[47]

What has been less obvious than the cultural nationalism of the Irish-Ireland movement is that it bears true witness to the reality of the *de facto* state established by Parnell. It has hardly been noticed, for example, that the various dissenting groups, which made up the heterogeneous movement, were actually a newly emerged opposition, and like all such oppositions in a one-party system, they were forced to legitimize themselves by claiming to represent a higher patriotism and a more wholesome national ideal than did the prevailing consensus of leader, party, and bishops. Thus their cultural nationalism, though abstractly sincere, served as a very useful cover in securing for them that ideological toleration so necessary to their political survival. That is why Sinn Fein was able to emerge eventually as the successor to the party and why Eamon de Valera succeeded John Redmond as leader. For within the framework of the consensus that was basic to the *de facto* Irish state, Sinn Fein evolved what was really the only viable alternative constitutional policy.[48] Sinn Fein argued that instead of having the Irish state made as legal as it was then real through the medium of the Liberal-Nationalist alliance in the House of Commons, the Irish representatives should withdraw from Westminster, set up a parliament in Dublin, and unilaterally declare the *de facto* state *de jure*. In presenting its policy of abstention, however, Sinn Fein was not simply offering the nation an alternative to the policy of the party. It was arguing that abstention was the only viable means for achieving the nation's end—a legally established state. The party's policy, Sinn Fein further argued, was in effect bankrupt, and the party must not merely give way, but it must give up. In a word, in what was essentially a one-party system, there was no room for another party or alternative leaders or policies. The task of Sinn Fein, therefore, was to win the nation's mandate, destroy the party, and thereby take its legitimate place in the consensus.

Before the Church consented, however, to the transfer of power, the bishops had to be convinced that Sinn Fein and its leader respected the bishops' place in the consensus and would come to terms with what was, in effect, the Irish political system rather than attempt to restructure it. The political conversion of the bishops as a body was a slow and painful process, and this explains both why the triumph of Sinn Fein was so long in coming and why it was so complete when it finally came.[49] Though a significant number of the bishops over the years had become disenchanted with the party for various reasons, the vast majority in early 1917 still supported the party, especially if the alternative was Sinn Fein. When in the spring of 1917, Lloyd George, for example, approved the calling of a convention, representing all shades of Irish political opinion, to recommend to his government a solution to the problem of self-government based on a "substantial agreement," the bishops as a body agreed to participate and named four representatives. The dilemma faced not only by those individual bishops disenchanted with the party, but by even those who had become outspoken supporters of Sinn Fein policy, was best expressed by the bishop of Limerick, Edward Thomas O'Dwyer, when writing Michael O'Riordan, the rector of the Irish College in Rome. "At our meeting this week," O'Dwyer reported on June 22, 1917, "we nominated 4 bishops for Convention: Cashel, Ross, Raphoe, and Down and Connor, all staunch '*Party*' men." "I agreed on the ground," he added, explaining his difficulty, "that, if we refused, the Gov't. might drop the whole thing, and then say that the Cath. bishops killed H. Rule." "It is a pity," he lamented, "that as a body we are not more independent."[50]

The bishops as a body, in fact, continued to support the party under the terms of the clerical-nationalist alliance until there was indeed no hope left for the party. Even in the face of a series of successive disasters for it in the first half of 1918—the failure of the convention, the death of John Redmond, the destruction of the Liberal-Nationalist alliance through the attempt to enforce conscription in Ireland, and the wholesale arrests of the Sinn Fein leadership on the flimsiest charges of a treasonous pro-German conspiracy— the bishops as a body still held on to their alliance with the party. As late as November the champion of the party among the bishops for nearly twenty years, Patrick O'Donnell, the bishop of Raphoe, was still prepared to sink or swim with it. "Sinn Fein," he complained to O'Riordan in Rome on November 24, 1918, "has placed Ireland under the feet of Prussianism: and yet, because of the executions following Easter Week the duplicity of the Government and the mistakes of the Irish Party, it is quite likely that Sinn Fein will sweep the country at the general elections." "Good men think they are having," he added, "a fling at England when they claim a Republic and say they will not go next or near her Parliament." "They will see soon but too late," O'Donnell noted very perceptively, "that abstention leads inevitably to partition." "They will also see," he further explained, "that whatever our rights the claim now for a Republic can be used everywhere as reason for not granting autonomy, in-as-much as autonomy is not asked and the concession of it to those who go for a Republic would be playing into the hands of men bent on disturbing the peace of the world." "These are the dangers," he concluded, "in allowing Sinn Fein a walk over at the elections."[51]

Less than two weeks later, however, even O'Donnell's political will had been sapped, and he wrote John Dillon, who had succeeded Redmond as leader, asking him to allow Sinn Fein the "walk over" he had deplored to O'Riordan. Dillon refused and courageously replied that duty and honor required no surrender.[52] The day after the election, when it was apparent to all that Sinn Fein had swept the country, O'Donnell again wrote O'Riordan in Rome. "There is," he sadly explained on December 16, 1918, "no measure of freedom that I would not desire for Ireland. It is only a question of the means." "May God bless the new leaders," O'Donnell added, accepting the new order, "who at a critical time take up a heavy load of responsibility." "The priests," he then reported, and referring to his clergy's part in the South and West Donegal elections, "acted splendidly. Beyond the public expression of my views, I did not interfere. The priests were free as far as I was concerned. But they either supported the Party or kept silent in public."[53] Another of those "staunch" supporters of the party at the convention in 1917 also wrote O'Riordan shortly after the election. "The Sinn Feiners," Joseph McRory, the bishop of Down and Connor, wrote from Belfast, "as you know, have swept the country." "It is a marvelous triumph for *Sinn Fein*," McRory then noted, "but the country is thoroughly and intelligibly tired of the Party." "It was time," he added for good measure, "to put an end to it."[54]

What made it easier for the great majority of the bishops who had previously supported the party to acquiesce in the Sinn Fein triumph was that they had become convinced, however slowly, that the new party and its leader posed no real threat to their power or their influence. The bishop of Killaloe, Michael Fogarty, for example, had written O'Riordan shortly after the Easter Rising and made what indeed would be in time the crucial distinction for all the bishops. "There are," Fogarty explained on June 16, 1916, "Sinn Fein, & Sinn Fein—those on for rebellion, those short of that in pursuit of Irish ideals, religion, moral social etc. The former were few, the great body belonged to the latter class." "Practically all Irish Ireland," he added, "has gone over since the rebellion to this latter class." "That is," Fogarty explained further, "they don't want rebellion, but the brutal shooting and deportation of these young insurgents after surrender has filled the country with indignation and roused such an anti-English feeling as I never saw before!"[55] When more than two years later Sinn Fein destroyed the party in the general election, the great majority of the bishops, whatever they believed about the wisdom of Sinn Fein's policy of abstention, had apparently come to the same conclusion as the bishop of Killaloe concerning the religious and moral probity of the members and adherents of the new party.

Shortly after the elections O'Riordan, in order obviously to forestall any effort on the part of the British government to secure a Roman condemnation of Sinn Fein, shrewdly canvassed the opinions of a large number of the Irish bishops as to the soundness of the new party. The bishops who replied were all obviously of one mind. "The Sinn Feiners of my diocese," the bishop of Galway, Thomas O'Dea, reassured O'Riordan on March 9, 1919, "are the very reverse of anti-clerical or anti-religious. As a body they are ardent Catholics. Many of them I know intimately & from my own knowledge can bear this testimony of them."[56] Even among those bishops who had opposed them in the general election, Sinn Fein found those who would bear witness. "The Sinn Feiners," the bishop of Ferns, William Codd, assured O'Riordan from Wexford on March 16, "are not different from the rest of the people as Catholics. They are quite good and practical Catholics. They are not anti-clerical, they have many clerical adherents with us. And nothing could be said against them, lay or clerical, as regards temperance."[57]

But of all the bishops who replied, the bishop of Kildare and Leighlin, Patrick Foley, perhaps best summed it all up in a long, interesting, and perceptive letter. "As to your query respecting the young men of my Diocese, who belong to the Sinn Fein organization," Foley explained to O'Riordan on March 21, 1919, from Carlow, "I can say without the slightest hesitation that as a body they are most exemplary in attending to their religious duties and living good, Christian lives." "From conversations which I frequently had with them here," he reported, "I am satisfied that they are quite willing to accept the teaching of the Church, even when it may not be quite in harmony with some of their views for instance the lawfulness of the Easter Rising for the success of which there was no hope whatever."

> But, while stating this, I think it only right to add that the Anti-Conscription movement was the occasion of a most impressive religious movement in all parts of the country: all classes, young and old, rich & poor, no matter [the] brand of politics they favoured crowded the churches day after day and week after week, and displayed the most marvelous fervour in prayer, reception of the Sacraments, assisting at Mass etc. that had ever occurred in the country. No mission that was ever held so profoundly affected the lives of the whole Catholic people, and the Sinn Feiners were second to no others.
>
> There has been an outbreak of crime here and there within the past few months. In my own Diocese, the raids for arms were few, and there was no outrage connected with them; but we have had incendiarism in four or five cases—a crime which had been utterly unheard

of up to a few months ago, and which I believe is not yet at an end. It is only the extreme wing of the Sinn Fein movement from whom any such real danger is likely to arise. The remnant of the Citizen Army in Dublin has become very active, and although it has not yet got the upper hand, it is causing great trouble to the moderate men among the Sinn Fein leaders.[58]

Foley then went on to explain that there was a great disappointment among the Sinn Fein rank and file in President Wilson, who they hoped would favor Ireland's right to self-determination at the peace conference. Foley expected that the disappointment would lead to further trouble from the extreme elements, and for that reason he wished that de Valera, who had been arrested on the charge of promoting a pro-German conspiracy, and was just about to be released from jail, would return and take "supreme charge of the whole movement." "He made," Foley confessed of de Valera, "a great impression on me at Maynooth last April when I had a talk with him as well as the advantage of hearing what he said at the Conference with the Bishops."

> He did not say much; he is not an orator, and never will be, but he impressed me very deeply with the great sense of responsibility which he evidently felt attached to his position in the tremendous crisis which existed at the time. He is transparently honest, sincere, and courageous; but he has a very big burden to bear and his position needs a man of very great parts.

"I need hardly say," Foley further confessed, "that I have no hope whatever of seeing an 'independent Republic' established." "If we could get," he then added hopefully, "full control of all taxation, of customs, excise and relief from the intolerable burden of war taxation it would be as much as could be hoped for from the present govt." "The Tory elements which predominate," Foley finally prophesied in conclusion, "would not haggle as much over this as the radical cabinet elements but they will not compel the N.East corner."[59]

When the British government objected, however, to Sinn Fein unilaterally declaring the Irish state to be as legal as it was then real, Sinn Fein in the name of the new national consensus declared itself ready to submit the question to the arbitrament of force. The result of that submission was the emergence of an Irish Free State in 1921. When the Sinn Fein party then split on the question of whether the Irish state was to be a republic or a dominion, the

Church threw the weight of its power and influence to the side of the constitutional majority. In doing so the Church was simply fulfilling the obligations it had contracted in 1884 when the Irish state was being born. As long as the party in the state fulfilled its part of the agreement and was the legitimate party sanctioned by the nation, the Church could in fact do no less. That is why in the ensuing civil war among the Sinn Fein guardians, the bishops in a joint pastoral in early October 1922 formally declared against Eamon de Valera and his republicans.[60] They did so not because de Valera or his followers posed any real threat to their own power and influence, but because he, like Parnell thirty years before, no longer retained the confidence of the majority of the party and was, therefore, no longer the legitimate leader. De Valera's further attempt to assert his leadership and to claim legitimacy for the minority of the party in the system of consensus was then resisted by the bishops as being patently unconstitutional. When he, however, succeeded to power in 1932, the bishops could consistently welcome him and his new Fianna Fail party—as indeed they had accepted John Redmond and the reunited Irish party ten years after the fall of Parnell—as the legitimate guardians because he and his new party were constitutionally endorsed by a majority and still posed no threat to the Church's place in the state. De Valera, in fact, went so far as to make that informal concordat of 1884 more explicit in the constitution he drew up for the Irish state and had ratified by the nation in 1937.

The ascendancy of Eamon de Valera and his Fianna Fail party for some thirty years after 1932 is simply a conclusive testimony to the uniqueness and durability of the political system conceived by O'Connell and consolidated by Parnell. De Valera's own political greatness certainly owes much to his understanding of the dynamics of this system of politics by consensus. He was not only the leader and Fianna Fail the party, but he has also always been scrupulously correct about the prerogatives of the bishops as a body in the consensus. Implicit in the Parnellite concordat with the bishops was a constitutional division of labor or responsibility. The leader and the party retained the rights of initiative and determination with regard to the Home Rule and land questions, while the bishops retained control over education. By 1910 the land and education questions had been settled, and when the Irish Free State was finally ratified by treaty in 1921, the last of the specific objectives of the

Parnellite program was achieved. By 1921, therefore, where the rights of initiative and determination with regard to national policy lay became somewhat more subjective.

The constitutional division of labor, however, which was still basic to the consensus, remained real. In the new Free State the old objectives represented by Home Rule and the land question were broadened to include all that was essentially political and economic, while the Church expanded its acknowledged prerogative in education into other social areas. The justification for such an extension of power and influence on the part of the Church, of course, was rooted in its claim that it was responsible for the moral well-being of the nation. Moreover, the governments of Liam Cosgrave before 1932 and afterward of de Valera freely acknowledged that it was the duty of the state to help maintain traditional Catholic teaching and values. If Cosgrave, for example, refused to legalize divorce or to allow the dissemination of birth control information and censored films and books, de Valera made divorce unconstitutional, banned the import or sale of contraceptive devices, and regulated dance halls, besides incorporating Catholic teaching on the family, education, and private property in the 1937 constitution.[61]

On the other hand, de Valera has demonstrated time and again that he understands the limits of the bishops' rights within the consensus. He has been most careful in maintaining both his and his party's authority when challenged either individually or collectively by the bishops. When there was some individual criticism by bishops of his policy of "economic war" with Britain in the early 1930s, he studiously and rightly ignored them. He refused, moreover despite considerable Catholic pressure, either to outlaw the Communist party or to recognize the Franco regime in Spain. During the Second World War his government actually censored an episcopal pastoral because it conflicted with the stated official policy of neutrality. More important than all these, however, was his and his party's refusal in the 1940s to implement what amounted to Catholic proposals for the vocational organization of the state and a basic overhaul of social services.[62] The resistance to such proposals by de Valera and his party was rooted in the concept of "ministerial responsibility." This was to say that if the state were basically reorganized or the social services fundamentally reformed, the rights of initiative and determination with regard to such measures would remain with the leader and the party and not with the bishops. An important limit was thus set on the rights of the bishops in expanding their power and influence in the social area. Finally, de Valera's real political astuteness with regard to the rights of the bishops within the consensus was demonstrated once again in the early 1950s by his delicate handling of the controversial maternal and child welfare, or "mother and child," scheme. His timely private intervention prevented the bishops from making fools of themselves publicly and thus diluting, if not actually jeopardizing, their own power and influence within the consensus.[63] De Valera's real achievement in Church-state relations, however, cannot be fully appreciated if it is not understood that while he has done much to make the Irish state more confessional, he has also prevented it from becoming any more clerical.

The foundations for that confessional state were laid, of course, by Daniel O'Connell. In setting up the fundamental alliance between Church and nation in his attempt to create an Irish state, O'Connell, though unsuccessful, structured a political frame that has constrained all his successors in Irish politics. In joining Church to nation he not only made their future both more certain and secure, but more sane, for he provided thereby for the effective containment of the most violent aspects of the nation's personality as represented by the Young Ireland, Fenian, and republican Sinn Fein tradition. The price he paid for that containment was the integration of the Church in an inextricable way into the pattern of constitutional politics. What O'Connell did not foresee, and what he could not have known, was that the Church in the generation after his death was going to build itself socially and economically into the very vitals of the nation until it became virtually at one with the nation's identity and an essential part of its consciousness. The result, of course, was to make the state, when it finally emerged under Parnell, much more exclusively Catholic.

By providing the nation with its shield and defense in the Irish state, furthermore, Parnell assured the nation that the issue was no longer survival but fulfillment. Like O'Connell, however, Parnell was also a supreme realist in that by imaginatively taking up the material at hand he did not attempt to make of that material more than was possible. He understood, for example, that since the emerging state was essentially Catholic, the Church would have to be accommodated if that state was ever to become a functioning political reality. Though he realized it was possible to coerce the Church through the Catholic tenant farmers qua nation, his real genius lay in his further understanding that the effectiveness of that tactic must decline with its use. His strategy, therefore, was to court the Church constitutionally and eventually come to terms with her in an informal but effective concordat. The price Parnell paid in turn for the accommodation of the Church, of course, was to make his *de facto* Irish state essentially a confessional one. Finally, it was left to de Valera to make that state as formally confessional as it has been informally so since 1886.

The ability to distinguish between a confessional and a clerical state, then, is necessary to any understanding of the nature and extent of the power and influence of the Church in modern Ireland. The nature and extent of the power of the Church are really a function of its acknowledged rights and prerogatives within the political consensus, while the nature and extent of its influence are certainly dependent on the confessional character of the state. In other words, because the power of the Church is constitutionally limited and the influence of the Church is constrained by traditional political values that are as deeply rooted in the historical memory as the traditional Catholic values, Ireland is not a clerical state. This confessional rather than clerical character of the Irish state explains why the Church has never been faced with a serious anticlerical movement. Fenians, Parnellites, and Republicans, for example, have all complained that the Church was exceeding the limits of its legitimate power and influence in condemning them, but they have never dared to go so far as to maintain the Church had no claim to power and influence in Ireland. They did not go that far because they could not, and they could not because the Church had so integrated itself psychologically, functionally, and historically into the Irish way of life that it became virtually at one with the nation's identity. In the last analysis, then, the considerable power and influence of the Church in Ireland have remained real because the Church has never attempted to turn what has been a confessional state for nearly a hundred years into a clerical one and has loyally accepted its unique constitutional place in that state.

NOTES

[1] Emmet Larkin, "Economic Growth, Capital Investment, and the Roman Catholic Church in Nineteenth-Century Ireland," *AHR*, 72 (1966–67): 852–84; Larkin, "The Devotional Revolution in Ireland, 1850–75," *AHR*, 77 (1972): 625–52.

[2] Raymond D. Crotty, *Irish Agricultural Production: Its Volume and Structure* (Cork, 1966). See in particular chapter 1 for a most thoughtful and illuminating account of

Irish economic conditions, and especially the emergence of the tenant farmer class, in the late seventeenth and early eighteenth centuries.

[3] This is a conservative estimate. It is calculated on the basis that there were in Ireland in 1861 some 158,000 holdings of more than thirty acres. This figure is then reduced by five per cent in order to distinguish occupiers from holders, and the result is 150,000 occupiers. This latter figure is further reduced by estimating that thirty per cent of the occupiers were Protestants, which then results in a figure of 105,000 Roman Catholic occupiers of more than thirty acres. If the number of occupiers are then counted as heads of families, and the number in a family is calculated at five, the figure arrived at is roughly 500,000. While the figure of five per cent in reducing holders to occupiers appears reasonable in light of the available evidence, the figure of thirty per cent for Protestant occupiers may be too high, since Protestants made up about twenty per cent of the population. Still, given the long-term privileged position and greater wealth of the Protestant community, it is more prudent to overestimate than to underestimate their numbers as occupiers. In any case, 500,000 appears a reasonable working figure because it is certainly a lower limit, and more especially so in the years after the famine. The numerical strength of this class was, of course, enhanced by its cousinhood in the cities and towns. Given, however, the current state of quantitative research in Irish social history, any estimate of its numbers must be, at best, an educated guess. If the some 80,000 first- and second-class houses enumerated in the 1861 census containing one family in civic areas, as distinguished from rural areas, are multiplied by five, the number of this urban cousinhood is about 400,000. If only half of them were Roman Catholics, some 200,000 then may be added to the 500,000 for a grand total of 700,000 for this class in 1861. That this is a minimal estimate and that the total was undoubtedly greater are obvious, but given the current state of knowledge, as has been pointed out, it is more sensible at this stage to understate the case. See *Census of Ireland, 1861* (Dublin, 1864), pt. 5, pp. xv–xix, for the definition of what constituted a family and first- and second-class houses and page 462 for the numbers of first- and second-class houses containing one family. Finally, a word must be said about the geographical distribution of this more than thirty acre tenant farmer class. The assumption that has been made here, of course, is that the overall distribution of the Protestants and Catholics who made up this class was even. Since this is patently not so and since the Protestant farmers holding more than thirty acres were undoubtedly concentrated in the six counties that today make up Northern Ireland, the political significance of the same class of Catholics in the south is considerably enhanced, especially so as the electorate was expanded in the course of the nineteenth century. The implications for the progressive polarization of the two communities, north and south, are obvious.

[4] F. S. L. Lyons, *Ireland since the Famine* (New York, 1971), 22. See also Crotty, *Irish Agricultural Production*, 64, and L. M. Cullen, *An Economic History of Ireland since 1660* (New York, 1972), 100–04.

[5] W. A. Maguire, *The Downshire Estates in Ireland, 1801–1845* (Oxford, 1972), 119.

[6] John O'Donovan, *The Economic History of Livestock in Ireland* (Dublin, 1940), 212–13. See also Crotty, *Irish Agricultural Production*, 57–58. There are no reliable figures for livestock population in Ireland before the famine, but the export of live animals to England gives some idea of the apparent increase in numbers. In 1800, for example, Ireland exported 17,984 live cattle, 1,671 live sheep, and 4,169 live pigs, while in 1848 the respective numbers were 190,828, 279,706, and 232,674. See Crotty, *Irish Agricultural Production*, table 65 B, p. 277.

[7] Joseph Lee, "The Ribbonmen," in T. Desmond Williams, ed., *Secret Societies in Ireland* (Dublin, 1973), 34. Professor Lee emphasizes the role of the laborers and cottiers vis-à-vis the tenant farmers and the landlords, but most of the evidence he adduces would serve as well for the marginal farmers and their sons who were well on their way to becoming either laborers, cottiers, or emigrants.

[8] James A. Reynolds, *The Catholic Emancipation Crisis in Ireland, 1823–1829* (New Haven, 1954).

[9] L. J. McCaffrey, *Daniel O'Connell and the Repeal Year* (Lexington, 1966), 211–213.

[10] John B. Broderick, *The Holy See and the Irish Movement for the Repeal of the Union with England, 1829–1847* (Rome, 1951), 45–50. See also, for example, William Kinsella, bishop of Ossory, who wrote to the rector of the Irish College in Rome, Christopher Boylan, from Kilkenny on January 3, 1831: "Mr. O'Connell is agitating the question of repealing the union—the people of property & respectability are all opposed to him, and the Government are determined to put him down as they say his object is rebelling against the authority of the King of England. All the Irish Bishops unanimously resolved, and published their resolution of not permitting the Priests to preach from the altar on political affairs. This I announced six months ago in public conference: and yesterday a Capuchin Friar in this City preached at Mass on the repeal of the Union, and stigmatised every man who would not join in this mad attempt." Paul Cullen Papers, Archives of the Irish College, Rome.

[11] Broderick, *Holy See and the Irish Movement*, 59.

[12] *Ibid.*, 113, and see also Oliver MacDonagh. "The Politicization of the Irish Catholic Bishops, 1800–1850," *Historical Journal*, 18 (1975): 37–53. MacDonagh notes that nineteen of twenty-nine bishops were "at one stage or other open repealers' (p. 47, n.28). The figure of twenty-nine, however, is somewhat inflated because, in effect, he counts the bishops of Derry and Galway twice. John MacLaughlin, the bishop of Derry, became insane in 1845, and Edward Maginn was appointed his administrator. While it is true that both were Repealers, they really should not be counted individually in that MacLaughlin never recovered from his illness. George J. P. Browne, the bishop of Galway, was translated to the diocese of Elphin in early 1844 to succeed Patrick Burke who died in late 1943. Browne was himself succeeded in Galway by Laurence O'Donnell. Though Burke, Browne, and O'Donnell were all Repealers, only two of them were bishops at any one time, and they should, therefore, be counted as two instead of three. MacDonagh also lists Kinsella, the bishop of Ossory, as an "open repealer." Kinsella, however, does not appear to have ever joined the Repeal Association and publicly eschewed politics, though he indeed admitted that personally he favored repeal and permitted his priests to be members of the association. I, therefore, take the number of Irish bishops at any one time in this period to be twenty-seven and the number who formally joined the Repeal Association to be sixteen. The real issue among the bishops as I understand it was not perhaps repeal or no repeal, but rather to what extent the bishops thought the clergy should be involved in politics.

[13] McCaffrey, *Daniel O'Connell*, 212–39.

[14] Angus Macintyre, *The Liberator: Daniel O'Connell and the Irish Party, 1830–1847* (London, 1965), 126–29.

[15] Reynolds, *Catholic Emancipation Crisis*, 14–30.

[16] Oliver MacDonagh, "The Contribution of O'Connell," in Brian Farrell, ed., *The Irish Parliamentary Tradition* (Dublin, 1973), 164–65.

[17] See, for example, the correspondence of the venerable and influential archbishop of Dublin, Daniel Murray, who led the opposition among the bishops to the political and ecclesiastical policies of Archbishop MacHale and who wrote to Paul Cullen, rector of the Irish College in Rome, complaining of MacHale's alter ego, the bishop of Ardagh and Clonmacnoise: "Doctor Higgins has brought us into sad trouble by a very intemperate speech which he made at a Repeal dinner in Mullingar. He not only declared that all the Bishops in Ireland are ardent Repealers but that they participate in every sentiment which he uttered one of which was that he owed nothing to any Aristocrat, save the *unbounded contempt* that he had *for the whole class*, and another of which was that if the Meetings of the Union were prevented from being held in the open fields we would retire to our Chapels, and *suspend all other*

instruction, in order to devote all our time to teaching the people to be Repealers. I was obliged in my own defense to declare that I have taken no part whatever in the great political movement which is agitating the Country. I am sure that political agitation of this kind will not be considered at Rome as the fittest occupation of Bishop. Could anything be prudently done there to restrain us somewhat more within the sphere of our immediate duties? Could any private admonition to that effect be prudently given? The whole Country is kept in a state of ferment for the purpose of obtaining an object, which the Govt declares will be resisted even at the hazard of Civil War. And yet many of the Clergy and even several of the Bishops (no doubt for good, but I believe very mistaken motives) are keeping alive this dangerous excitement. In the meantime the Govt is alarmed, and is looking with great anxiety at the part that our Clergy are acting. I believe that it is an unwise part; and that if they were more deeply imbued with horror for the calamities which ensued from the French Revolution and the Irish Insurrection they would be slow to adopt it." May 5, 1843, Cullen Papers.

[18] The correlation between O'Connell's parliamentary strength and the area where the Roman Catholic tenant farmers who held more than thirty, and especially more than one hundred, acres predominated is evident. If a line is drawn, for example, from Galway city on the west coast, north and east to the port town of Dundalk, on the east coast, the area south of the line is O'Connell's political stronghold and the home of the more than thirty acre Catholic tenant farmers. For the representation pattern of O'Connell's political strength, see Macintyre, *Liberator: Daniel O'Connell*, app. D, following page 309. For the geographical distribution of the more than thirty acre Catholic tenant farmers, see T. W. Freeman, *Ireland: A General and Regional Geography* (London, 1969), fig. 32, p. 184. See also Ruth Dudley Edwards, *An Atlas of Irish History* (London, 1973), 170.

[19] Given the meager amount of work done in Irish social history to date, it is of course impossible as yet to prove in any statistically conclusive way the financial, numerical, and devotional importance of the strong tenant farmers as a class to the Irish Church. Still, when all the evidence is in, I do not think the picture will appreciably change from what it is now possible to construct with the evidence available. Even a brief perusal, for example, of the three volumes of Peader MacSuibhne's *Paul Cullen and His Contemporaries* (Kildare, 1961–65) will make clear the importance of the strong tenant farmers to the Church. The letters to Paul Cullen in the Irish college in Rome from his family also give a good picture of the abilities and values of the cream of the Catholic tenant farmer class. The extended family was very often financially mobilized in the interests of both Cullen and the college of which he was rector. His brother Thomas, for example, wrote him from Liverpool that "after you had written to Mick some time since stating that your cash was running low we applied to Uncle Pat to agitate a little amongst the friends in Meath to make up five Hundred pounds to send you." Thomas went on to explain that the death of Uncle William, who left a very large family, had "upset the project," but that they had then resolved among themselves to make up £250. "You might well thank Peter," Thomas concluded, "for his portion of £60—a like sum from me and £130 from Mick." Sept. 8, 1837, Cullen Papers. Or again, Thomas wrote enclosing £200 and included the names of the contributors so that they might be properly thanked: "Pat Maher—50 [?], 10, Thomas Maher 30, Mrs. Whelan 10, Mrs. Wood 10, My mother 10, Edw Cullen 10 & c—70." Apr. 8, 1840, Cullen Papers. For an interesting discussion of the contribution of the tenant farmer class to the composition of the Irish clergy, see K. H. Connell, *Irish Peasant Society* (Oxford, 1968), 123–26. See also John Healy, *Maynooth College: Its Centenary History* (Dublin, 1895), 366–67, and Raynolds, *Catholic Emancipation Crisis*, 45. For a discussion of the incidence of religious practice before the famine, see the important article by David W. Miller, "Catholic Religious Practice in Pre-Famine Ireland," *Journal of Social*

History, 8 (1975). There seems to be a real correlation between the higher incidence of attendance at mass and the area of O'Connellite representation that was dominated by the more than thirty acre tenant farmer class. The correlation is even more convincing between the high incidence of mass attendance and the towns that returned O'Connellites to Parliament and where the Catholic shopkeepers and £10 householders were in the ascendancy.

²⁰ See Healy, *Maynooth College*, 370, and also "Complete List of Prelates Educated at Maynooth," 631–34. Twenty of the twenty-seven Irish bishops in 1850 were educated at Maynooth. See also app. 13, pp. 729–30. For example, from 1845, when the Maynooth grant was increased by Peel, until January 1, 1871, when the grant was withdrawn with compensation in consequence of disestablishment all around in 1869, there were some 500 free places on the public foundation. There were also some 25 free places available on private foundations at Maynooth (p. 726) for a grand total of 525 free places. The number of students at Maynooth, however, always exceeded the number of free places because of those who could, partially or fully, pay their own way. Before the increase in the parliamentary grant in 1845, when there were only some 275 free places that were publicly and privately endowed, there were more than 400 students, and in 1895, when there were still some 368 free places, there were 614 students attending Maynooth.

²¹ Aiden Devereaux to Paul Cullen, Sept. 19, 1836, Cullen Papers.

²² Healy, *Maynooth College*, 283–84.

²³ Reynolds, *Catholic Emancipation Crisis*, 46.

²⁴ Thomas Cullen to Paul Cullen, May 20, 1843, Cullen Papers.

²⁵ *Ibid.*

²⁶ Charles W. Russell to Paul Cullen, Aug. 28, 1843, *ibid.*

²⁷ Russell to Cullen, Sept. 24, 1843, *ibid.*

²⁸ Cullen to David Moriarty, Oct. 7, 1860, William Monsell Papers, National Library of Ireland, Dublin, box 8,319.

²⁹ Cullen to Tobias Kirby, Tobias Kirby Papers, Archives of the Irish College, Rome.

³⁰ Cullen to Moriarty, Sept. 19, 1867, Monsell Papers.

³¹ Cullen's insistence on episcopal control over education was so consistent that he would not even tolerate other forms of clerical control. For example, in 1877 the Irish Christian Brothers, a very large Catholic teaching order, appealed to Rome about the statutes concerning them, which had been passed among the many at the Synod of Maynooth in 1875 by the Irish bishops for the good governance of the Irish Church. In their memorial to Rome the brothers had asked that the bishops and parish priests be excluded from examining in their schools in secular subjects, but they were willing to allow them to examine their pupils in catechism. "Their pretensions on this score," Cullen complained to Laurence Gillooly, the bishop of Elphin, on January 29, 1878, when Rome forwarded him the brothers' memorial for his reply, "are much higher than those of the government. The National Board allows the P.P.'s as managers to examine in everything." Laurence Gillooly Papers, Archives of the Diocese of Elphin, Sligo. A few days later Cullen informed Kirby in Rome that he and the bishops of his province had drawn up a reply for propaganda and, "I think it is made quite clear that nihil innovandum est." Feb. 1, 1878, Kirby Papers.

³² E. R. Norman, *The Catholic Church and Ireland in the Age of Rebellion 1859–1873* (London, 1965), 86–132.

³³ James O'Leary to Kirby, Dec. 7, 1865, Kirby Papers.

³⁴ William Keane to Kirby, Feb. 6, 1866, *ibid.*

³⁵ For an interesting discussion of Fenianism as a class movement, see Malcolm Brown, *The Politics of Irish Literature* (London, 1972), 155–57. See also Cullen's remark to Kirby describing the situation in Dublin: "The poor have not joined the broth-

erhood of S.P. [St. Patrick]—the brothers are a degree higher—tradesmen and mechanics who read the newspapers." Apr. 22, 1862, Kirby Papers.

[36] Cullen to Kirby, Apr. 6, 1862, Kirby Papers. "I sent you all sorts of papers about the brotherhood of S. Patrick. I fear it will do great mischief. The principles are most dangerous, and the design is to set the people against the priests." On enclosing £200 in Peter's Pence to Kirby on April 22, 1862, Cullen remarked, "Are not the poor very good—they give all—but the nasty secret societies wd soon destroy them." Again on May 9, 1862, Cullen explained to Kirby in Italian, "It is a very dangerous society, and it will become more dangerous because the members who are priests claim to have the approval of Monsignor MacHale. . . . I hope that our poor people will be saved from the danger of adopting the wicked maxims of Mazzini and Garibaldi." *Ibid.*

[37] Michael V. Hazel, "The Young Charles Stewart Parnell, 1874–1876," *Éire-Ireland*, 8 (1973):44–45.

[38] For the attitude of at least one of those Catholic tenant farmers, see the semiliterate letter of Denis Riordan to his brother Michael, a seminarian in the Irish College in Rome, on January 1, 1881 "I had settled with my Landlord before the agitation had become properly fruitful. Very probably but for the action of Mr. Parnell half the people would be ejected from their Homes, and inspite of the power of Landlord or Government he have stoped Eviction and reduced the rents to Griffet's valuation in many cases. Now for instance my father, who was paying £116—0—0, the[y] obliged to take £56—0—0 it being the valuation. There is a Land League in every parish in the County with the Priests in allmost all cases at the head of it. The county is at present in great excitement as Mr. Parnell T D Sullivan & twelve others are being procuted by the Government but we have great hopes the jury will not find them guilty as the charges are innocent ones, because he want to put down tyrants, I will not say any more on this subject, as I could not propery explain to you the good he has done for the Irish people and the terrible stroke he have given to the Landlord class." Michael O'Riordan Papers, Archives of the Irish College, Rome. For the ascendancy of the Land League, see Sir Robert Anderson, *Sidelights on the Home Rule Movement* (London, 1906), 110: "But no mere list of these crimes would convey an adequate impression of the horrors of the Land League rule in Ireland. In many districts terror reigned in every cottage home that refused allegiance to what was fitly called 'the *de facto* Government.'" See also the London *Times*, Apr. 3, 1882: "What the power of summarily arresting and keeping in custody suspected persons has accomplished is the overthrow of the system of lawlessness embodied in the Land League, which aspired to, and in August and September last had succeeded in, establishing a rival Government ·to that of the Queen throughout the greater part of Ireland. The supremacy of such a power would have been fatal to the authority of the Imperial Crown." Quoted in Henry Harrison, *Parnell Vindicated* (Dublin, 1931), app. C, p. 334. I am most grateful to Mr. William M. Murphy for calling both of these pieces of evidence to my attention.

[39] The situation was perhaps summed up best by the earl of Carnarvon, who when he wrote this long and statesmanlike memorandum for his cabinet colleagues on December 7, 1886, had been the lord lieutenant of Ireland in a caretaker Conservative government for six months: "As regards the condition of the country, agrarian crime and outrage have been and continue low. . . . Boycotting has been held in check, as I said it would be, and has diminished, though it is still very mischievous and capable of development. On the other hand, the National League has lost none of its power. It has, on the contrary, acquired a remarkable organization and force. The Roman Catholic Clergy, though with reluctance on the part of the Bishops and higher clergy have been drawn more and more under the influence of the National League and into the ranks of the Nationalist Party. The landlords seem in most districts hopelessly alienated from the tenants, and without influence. . . . To all this I must add that

there is a great development of the Secret Societies in the United States, an abundance of money subscribed, the closest communication existing between them and kindred Societies in Ireland, which though not active, are only waiting the signal to become so, and are every week growing more formidable. . . . I can see only three courses: (1) To propose nothing and do nothing, and wait till we are turned out by a combination of Liberals and Irish, which is a view I only mention to discard, (2) The adoption of some considerable, yet comparatively minor measures in the hopes of tiding over the difficulty till the Irish Party are disintegrated—which, by the way, let me say would not really settle the difficulty or, perhaps, much improve the case. A large scheme of higher education seemed, at one time, the most likely expedient in this direction. . . . But events have moved too fast, and I am afraid that the attempt now would be too late, mainly through the action of one man. The Archbishop of Dublin, it is clear, has made an alliance with Mr. Parnell; he has publicly declared against such settlement as I think we ought to make, and he has within the last few weeks, strange to say, apparently won over a majority of the Bishops. . . . (3) One last alternative remains, viz. to do something without committing ourselves as a Government to any course which might divide the Party. I wish my colleagues to consider whether it might not be possible to propose a Joint Committee of both Houses to consider the relations of Ireland and England, or the better government of Ireland, or some such general proposition, subject to the two following conditions, expressed in the most distinct language. 1. The supremacy and authority of the Crown. 2. The maintenance of the rights of minorities in religion and property. This would gain time, would educate the party and the country to a knowledge of the case, in which they are extraordinarily ignorant; would be constitutionally a very defensible course; would give a chance of moderate counsels prevailing, would receive the combined action of both parties; and would, if we failed to come to a conclusion through the fault of the Irish Party, leave us free to deal with the question in a much more decided manner—and all this without commiting the Government in the first instance to any definite proposals." Earl of Carnarvon Papers, Public Record Office, London, 30/6/55. When the cabinet opted indeed for the alternative Carnarvon mentioned only "to discard," he remarked to the Earl of Harrowby, Lord Privy Seal, "but a Cabinet is like a Council of War: it is very timid." Dec. 17, 1886, Carnarvon Papers.

[40] Emmet Larkin, *The Roman Catholic Church and the Creation of the Modern Irish State, 1878–1886* (Philadelphia, 1975).

[41] John MacEvilly to Kirby, Dec. 11, 1879, Kirby Papers.

[42] Michael V. Hazel, "Charles Stewart Parnell and the Creation of the Modern Irish State, 1874–1886" (Ph.D. dissertation, University of Chicago 1974), 285–89.

[43] Quoted in *Freeman's Journal* (Dublin), Oct. 2, 1884.

[44] MacEvilly, to Kirby, Oct. 26, 1884, Kirby Papers.

[45] Edwards, *Atlas of Irish History*, 171–73.

[46] David W. Miller, *Church, State and Nation in Ireland, 1898–1921* (Pittsburgh, 1973).

[47] Lyons, *Ireland since the Famine*, 219–42.

[48] Robert Kee, *The Green Flag: A History of Irish Nationalism* (London, 1972), 450–51.

[49] The various groups that made up the Irish-Ireland movement, it is interesting to note, were not only contemptuous of the party and its leader, but most of them also ran into difficulties with the clergy, high and low. The Gaelic League, in particular, had problems with the clergy. See Martin Waters, "Peasants and Emigrants: Considerations of the Gaelic League as a Social Movement," an unpublished paper, which gives a good account of the problems of the League with some of the local clergy. See also W. P. Ryan, *The Pope's Green Island* (London, 1912). Ryan, a prominent Gaelic Leaguer and Irish-Ireland enthusiast, and his newspaper, the *Irish Peasant*,

were anathematized by Michael Cardinal Logue, archbishop of Armagh. Ryan attempted to carry on, but the paper eventually collapsed and Ryan emigrated for a second time to London. The Irish labor movement also had its difficulties with the clergy. See Emmet Larkin, "Socialism and Catholicism in Ireland," *Church History,* *33* (1964): 462–83. The All for Ireland League, the Irish Agricultural Organization Society, the Gaelic Athletic Association, all had their contretemps with the clergy. Still, not one of these organizations may be described as anticlerical. What they actually wanted was room to challenge the political consensus. Since the Church was integral to that consensus, it was inevitable that they would quarrel with the clergy as they had with the leader and the party. There was in the period between 1900 and 1914, moreover, a large increase in the volume of literature criticizing the role of the Church in Irish society. The best examples of this kind of literature are the works of Michael J. McCarthy, which, if they prove nothing else, at least indicate there was a market for such work. See his *Five Years in Ireland, 1895–1900* (Dublin, 1901), *Priests and People in Ireland* (Dublin, 1903), and *Rome in Ireland* (London, 1904). A complete bibliography of such literature is of course impossible here, but some of the more prominent examples may be easily cited. Besides Ryan's *Pope's Green Island,* there are also F. H. O'Donnell's *The Ruin of Education in Ireland* (London, 1902) and *Paraguay on Shannon* (London, 1908). See also Filson Young, *Ireland at the Crossroads* (Dublin, 1906), R. J. Smith, *Ireland's Renaissance* (Dublin, 1903), and the novels of Gerald O'Donovan, in particular *Father Ralph* (London, 1913).

[50] Edward Thomas O'Dwyer to Michael O'Riordan, June 22, 1917, O'Riordan Papers.

[51] Patrick O'Donnell to O'Riordan, Nov. 24, 1918, *ibid.*

[52] Quoted in the correspondence between O'Donnell and John Dillon in F. S. L. Lyons, *John Dillon* (London, 1968), 449–51.

[53] O'Donnell to O'Riordan, Dec. 16, 1918. O'Riordan Papers.

[54] O'Donnell to O'Riordan, Nov. 26, 1918, *ibid.*

[55] Michael Fogarty to O'Riordan, June 16, 1916, *ibid.*

[56] Thomas O'Dea to O'Riordan, Mar. 9, 1919, *ibid.*

[57] William Codd to O'Riordan, Mar. 16, 1919, *ibid..*

[58] Patrick Foley to O'Riordan, Mar. 21, 1919, *ibid.*

[59] *Ibid.*

[60] Dorothy McArdle, *The Irish Republic* (Dublin, 1951), 701, 804.

[61] John H. Whyte, *Church and State in Modern Ireland, 1923–1970* (Dublin, 1971), 24–59.

[62] *Ibid.,* 96–119.

[63] *Ibid.,* 288–90.

Index

Abbey Theatre, 114.

Act of Union, 10, 43; effect on Irish Catholic electorate, 10; movement for repeal of, 96–97.

agriculture, Irish; golden age of, 15; depression, 15, 27; mainstay of Catholic middle classes, 17; Catholic share of agricultural sector, 34; decline of agricultural sector, 34; shift from tillage to grazing, 6, 9, 38, 100; statistics, 42, 93; supply of capital in, 3; farmer elite, 6–9; bourgeoisie, 9: proletariat, 9; agrarian secret societies, 108; harvest failures, 109; foreign competition, 109.

All for Ireland League, 114, 130 n. 49.

altar societies, 78.

Anstey, T. Chisholme, M.P. for Youghal, 66–68.

aristocracy; Protestant, 21–24; Irish, 24; English 24.

Australia; collections taken for Queenstown Cathedral, 27.

baptism; source of clerical income, 64, 67; clerical abuse of, 64, 67, 69, 80, 81.

Belgium, 13.

bishops, Irish Catholic, 9, 18, 20, 26, 28, 30, 31, 105; number in proportion to general population, 58–59; control over their priests, 62, 72–73, 77, 125 n. 10; Cullen gains control over, 73; and devotional exercises, 78; at Synod of Thurles, 79; Cullen promotes, 81; ultramontanism, 82; representative of clergy, 101; speak as a body for the Irish Church, 101; and education question, 106, 111–112, 120; attitudes toward Fenians, 107; in politics, 110–111; attitudes toward Land League, 110–111; attitudes toward British government, 111; and Roman Catholic Hierarchy, 111; and Irish Parliamentary party, 116, 117; secure clerical-nationalist alliance, 112; Sinn Fein, 117; limits on political power, 120–123; Repeal Association, 125 n. 10.

Boylan, Christopher, rector, Irish College in Rome, 125 n. 10.

British government, Catholic Church in Ireland borrows from, 24–25; impedes Irish economic growth, 35; Whig government, 97, 98; and Irish grievances, 97, 109; Radicals, 98; respect for power, 109; Gladstone's Liberal government, 110; Conservative government, 110; bishops lose confidence in, 111; education question, 112; and Sinn Fein, 116, 118, 119; opposition to O'Connell's repeal agitation, 125 n. 10.

Home Rule, need for Irish political party, 109; Gladstone's first bill, 110, 113; bishops and, 116; idea broadened, 121; responsibility of Irish political leader and party, 120.
House of Commons, see "Parliament."
Hynes, Eugene, 6.

income figures for Ireland, see "national income, Ireland."
Independent Orange Order, 114.
Industrial Revolution, in Belgium, 13; lack of in Ireland, 13, 91.
industry, 34.
Irish Agricultural Organizational Society, 114, 130 n. 40.
Irish Catholic Directory, 9, 74, 75.
Irish Catholicism, 1, 9, 91; national phenomenon, 108–109; see also "laity, Irish Catholic," and "Catholic Church in Ireland."
Irish Cavour Party, 105.
Irish Christian Brothers, 18, 19, 127 n. 31.
Irish identity, see "laity, Irish Catholic."
Irish-Ireland movement, 114–115, 129 n. 49.
Irish Labour Movement, 114.
Irish National League, 110.
Irish Parliamentary party, created, 98; securing Home Rule, 109, 110, 112; endorsed by bishops, 112, land question, 112; bishops and clergy select candidates, 112; and Irish state, 113; death of, 116–117.
Irish Republican brotherhood, see "Fenians."
Irish state, farmer elite and 96; O'Connell's efforts to create, 96–99; education vital to, 107; Church and Fenianism, 108–109; creation of 109–113; importance of bishops and clergy, 113; Parnell, 109–111, 113, 114; Sinn Fein, 115; Irish Free State, 35, 119–123; republic versus dominion, 119–120; Fianna Fail party, 120.
Irish Tenant League, 73.

Jesuits, 79.
Jones, Michael, C. C., Navan, Meath, 71.
Jubilee, see "Papal Jubilee."

Keane, William, Bishop of Cloyne, on Queenstown Cathedral, 26; on Fenians, 107.
Kearney, Thomas, P. P., diocese of Galway, 25.
Kelly, Michael, rector of Irish College in Rome, 31.
Kennedy, Liam, 4.
Kepple, John, P. P., Ballyhea, Charleville, 87 n. 29.
Kiernan, Michael, Archbishop of Armagh, 26.
Kilduff, John, Bishop of Ardagh and Clonmacnoise, 88.
Kingston, third Earl of, 21.
Kinsella, William, Bishop of Ossory; on Protestant aristocracy, 21; on O'Connell's Repeal Agitation, 125 n. 10.
Kirby, Tobias, rector, Irish College, Rome, 26, 28, 57, 78, 79, 106, 107, 111, 112, 87 n. 29, 89 n. 45.
Kyne, John, Catholic Chaplain at Alum Bagh, Lucknow, Oude, East India 87 n. 28.

labor, supply of, 15, 93; effect of Irish population on supply of, 93; poor house, 109; emigration, 109.
laity, Irish Catholic; identity crisis, 5–6, 82–83, nation's identity, 101; popular religion, 5–6; Devotional Revolution, 5–9, 57–85, 87 n. 21, 87 n. 29; farmer elite, 6–9, 92, 93, 96–99, 100–101, 113–114, 122, 124 n. 3, 126 n. 18, 126 n. 19; merchants, 16, 21, 24, 25, 99; smaller farmers, 21, 25, 99, 100, 108, 109; middle class, 24, 34–35; acquisition of land, 21, 25; size of, 27, 58–59, 77, 85 n. 7; share of Irish national income, 25, 27, 32–35; political power, 33; administrative power, 33; number in government and professions, 32–34; proportion at or below subsistence, 49; improved behavior, 63; secret societies to limit clerical avarice, 67–68; "respectable" class and Devotional Revolution, 72; growing awareness of sinfulness, 72; size of, 27, 58–59, 77, 85 n. 7; literacy, 85; grievances, 97, 109; poor ("ignorant") 108.